common core
Performance Coach™

(5)

English Language Arts

Performance Coach, English Language Arts, Grade 5   336NASE   ISBN-13: 978-1-62362-843-7   B
Cover Image: © Jeffrey Coolidge/Image Bank/Getty Images

Triumph Learning® 136 Madison Avenue, 7th Floor, New York, NY 10016

Printed in the United States of America.   10 9 8 7 6

CONTENTS

Standards

RL.5.2, RL.5.3, RL.5.4, RL.5.6, L.5.4.a

RL.5.2, RL.5.4, RL.5.5, RL.5.6, L.5.4.a, L.5.5.a

RL.5.2, RL.5.3, RL.5.4, RL.5.5, L.5.4.a, L.5.5.a, L.5.5.b

RL.5.2, RL.5.3, RL.5.9, L.5.4, L.5.4.a

RI.5.2, RI.5.5, L.5.4.b

RI.5.6, RI.5.8, RI.5.9, L.5.5.a

RI.5.4, RI.5.5, RI.5.6, RI.5.7, L.5.4.a, L.5.6

RI.5.4, RI.5.5, RI.5.6, RI.5.7, L.5.4.a, L.5.6

RI.5.2, RI.5.3, RI.5.4, RI.5.5, RI.5.6, RI.5.7, RI.5.9, L.5.6

RI.5.9, L.5.4.a, L.5.5.c

Standards

DEAR STUDENT

Welcome to *Performance Coach*!

We made this book to help you strengthen your reading, writing, and listening skills. These skills are important to have for every subject you study this year, not just English Language Arts.

Each lesson in this book has three parts:

GETTING THE IDEA ①

Review some of the basic concepts and skills you've already learned.

LESSON 1
Plot
Characters
Point of View

② COACHED EXAMPLE

Read a passage or two, then answer a set of questions. Don't worry—the questions have hints that will help you!

LESSON PRACTICE ③

Now you're on your own! This part contains a longer passage and additional questions to answer.

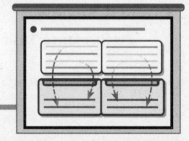

There are many different types of test items in *Performance Coach*. For some, you will have to choose more than one answer. For others, you will write out your answer. You will also see items that ask you to match words and phrases, put events in order, or complete a graphic organizer. Many items have more than one part. Be sure to read the directions carefully so you know how to answer each item.

HAVE A GREAT YEAR!

Sincerely,
TRIUMPH LEARNING

STRAND 1

Working with Literature

RL.5.2, RL.5.3, RL.5.4, RL.5.6, L.5.4.a

Fiction

① GETTING THE IDEA

Fiction is a type of writing about made-up people and events. You have probably read fiction in the form of a short story or a novel with chapters. The chart below identifies types of fiction.

Type of Fiction	What It's Like
contemporary fiction	takes place in the present day; includes realistic events and characters
historical fiction	takes place in the past; may involve people or events from history
science fiction	includes science and technology; may be set in the future, in space, or on another planet
fable	usually has animal characters and a moral, or lesson
myth	a traditional story from a certain place or people; may give reasons for how something in nature came to be

All fiction has the following elements: characters, setting, plot, point of view, and theme.

Characters
A **character** may be a person, or an animal or object with human-like qualities. Characters take part in the action of a story. A **character trait** can be what a character looks like or what his or her personality is like. Traits are revealed through characters' thoughts, words, and actions. Characters have **motivations**, or reasons behind their actions.

Looking at a character's traits and motivations can help you compare and contrast characters in the same story or characters in different stories.

Setting

The **setting** is where and when a story takes place. Sometimes you have to use story clues to figure out the setting. Read the following paragraph. Underline details that give you clues about the setting.

> Sophia stood on the upper deck, squinting toward the shore. Finally, she could see land. Far away, buildings seemed to rise from the water. Her long dress and shawl billowed in the wind.

Some stories have more than one setting. To compare settings within the same story, or between two stories, look at how details about time and place are different.

Plot

The **plot** is what happens in a story. It is made up of a series of events. A good plot has a **conflict**, or problem, the characters need to resolve. Conflict creates **suspense**, or excitement about what will happen next. Which sentences below reveal the conflict?

> Juan spent all summer training for a race. Then he tripped on the trail and took a painful fall. The doctor had bad news. Juan's leg was broken.

Point of View

Stories are told by **narrators**. A story's **point of view** is who is telling the story. A story in **first-person point of view** is told by a character in the story. The narrator uses the pronouns *I* and *me* when referring to himself or herself. Everything that happens in the story is seen through that character's eyes. A story in **third-person point of view** is told by someone outside the story. Because this narrator is not part of the story, readers see what happens to many characters.

A story can change, depending on who tells it. The passage below, adapted from "Little Red Riding Hood," is told from the wolf's point of view. How might it be different if told from Red Riding Hood's point of view?

> I was walking in the woods, starving, when a girl walked by. The smell from her basket made me drool. I tried to ask if she would share some food. But before I could say a word, she yelled and ran. She was so rude!

Theme

The **theme** is the message that an author wants readers to understand. An author does not usually state the theme. The reader has to figure it out by making an **inference** based on text evidence.

To figure out a story's theme, look at the challenges that the characters face and how the characters change. Read the passage summary below. What inference can you make about the passage's theme?

> Alice doesn't want to go visit her boring great-aunt Lil. She would rather be playing softball. Then Aunt Lil explains that she used to be a softball player, too. She shows Alice old pictures. Alice is fascinated.

Language Spotlight • Context Clues

Context clues are the words around an unfamiliar word that help you understand its meaning. When you read a word you don't know, look at other words in the sentence for help. Read the following sentences. Circle words that are clues to the meaning of the underlined word.

> Carrie knew that the uphill hike would not be easy, but it was even more grueling than she expected. Carrie was sweaty and tired by the time she finished.

How do the clue words help you understand the meaning of *grueling*? Use a dictionary to check the meaning.

Read the passage.

A Birthday Brainstorm

The excitement over my brother Milo's fourth birthday party faded when I realized something awful: it was the same day as Alma's sleepover! I had been looking forward to the sleepover for weeks, and now it seemed that I wouldn't be able to go. But after the bad news sank in, I decided I wouldn't tell Alma I couldn't go yet. There had to be a way for me to do both, so I searched my brain for a plan.

"We could move the party to Sunday," I said to Mom. "That way I can go to the sleepover Saturday, and I'd be home Sunday in plenty of time to help with the party."

Mom sighed and gave me an exasperated look. "Olivia, I've told you a million times that won't work because Aunt Marie and Uncle Will are driving in from out of town and they have to leave on Sunday."

OK, maybe I *had* brought up my plan a few times, but definitely not a million. Regardless, I wasn't ready to give up yet. I was intent on finding a way to be at Milo's party *and* Alma's sleepover.

"I've got it," I said one afternoon. "I won't come to the party, but I'll help you out a ton the week before. I'll make birthday decorations and bake and everything."

Mom touched my shoulder. "It's not just about helping me prepare for the party. I know you're disappointed, but Milo will be even more disappointed if you aren't at his party."

And that's when it hit me that I didn't want to miss out on Milo's party. He was my little brother, and it was important that I celebrate the day with him.

Unfortunately, my friends didn't make it easy for me to feel better about missing the sleepover. In the cafeteria the next day, the table buzzed with excitement as they talked about all the fun things they planned to do.

"You're so quiet, Olivia," Alma said. "Is everything OK?"

I sighed and said, "Not exactly. I can't go to your sleepover."

I explained about Milo's birthday, and Alma seemed to understand.

"Milo is an awesome little brother, and his party will definitely be fun," she said. "Remember the day I went to your house and he dressed up like a giraffe detective? We couldn't stop laughing." Alma told the story of Milo's giraffe detective, but I barely listened because in my head, the wheels were turning again.

After school, I ran through the house looking for Mom. "Mom, I have another idea," I said breathlessly. Mom, having lately heard many of my ideas, didn't look up from her computer. "No really," I continued, "this is a good one. My friends love Milo, so what if they come to his party, and after, my friends and I can go to Alma's house for the sleepover?"

Now Mom looked up. "You know what, that is a good idea. I'll even drive all of you to Alma's afterward."

Suddenly my anxious brain felt free and clear. Now I could focus on one thing: making sure Milo had a great birthday.

And that's exactly what happened. With so many people eager to help, we made tons of decorations and sang a really loud birthday song. Milo was thrilled with all the attention, and I was glad everything worked out so well.

Answer the following questions.

1 Underline **two** sentences that support the idea that Olivia is a determined person.

. . . But after the bad news sank in, I decided I wouldn't tell Alma I couldn't go yet. There had to be a way for me to do both, so I searched my brain for a plan.

"We could move the party to Sunday," I said to Mom. "That way I can go to the sleepover Saturday, and I'd be home Sunday in plenty of time to help with the party."

Mom sighed and gave me an exasperated look. "Olivia, I've told you a million times that won't work because Aunt Marie and Uncle Will are driving in from out of town and they have to leave on Sunday."

OK, maybe I *had* brought up my plan a few times, but definitely not a million. Regardless, I wasn't ready to give up yet. I was intent on finding a way to be at Milo's party *and* Alma's sleepover.

Hint How might someone show that he or she really wants something? Look for sentences in the story that show, through her words or actions, that Olivia is determined.

2 Which of these details from the passage tells the conflict?

   A. Olivia does not immediately tell Alma she can't go to the sleepover.

   B. Olivia tries to think of a way to go to Milo's party and the sleepover.

   C. Olivia realizes there are two important events on the same day.

   D. Olivia invites her friends to Milo's birthday party.

   E. Olivia goes to the sleepover after Milo's birthday party.

> **Hint** Remember that a conflict is a problem that a character or characters try to solve. You can usually find it at the beginning of a story. What is Olivia's problem?

3 Read the following sentence from the passage.

> **Alma told the story of Milo's giraffe detective, but I barely listened because in my head, the wheels were turning again.**

Explain what Olivia means when she says "in my head, the wheels were turning again."

_____

_____

_____

> **Hint** Think about what you know about Olivia. What has been her goal throughout this story? How has she been trying to solve her problem?

4 The following question has two parts. First, answer Part A. Then, answer Part B.

Part A

Which **best** states the theme of the passage?

A. Traditions keep families together.

B. If you don't give up, you may find a solution.

C. Friends should always come before family.

D. Home is where the heart is.

Part B

Which detail from the passage **best** supports the answer to Part A?

A. Olivia's mom expects Olivia to help with the party.

B. Milo's birthday is on the same day as Alma's sleepover.

C. Olivia's mom doesn't want to move the party to Sunday.

D. Olivia finds a way to go to both Milo's party and Alma's sleepover.

> **Hint** The theme is the message the author wants readers to understand. Details in the plot and the characters' actions give clues about theme. Think about Olivia's problem and how she overcomes it.

Use the Reading Guide to help you understand the passage.

Operation Robot Rescue

Reading Guide

What does Eli want to do with W-52? What does Hal want to do?

How does Hal get from place to place?

How does Eli get from his home to Hal?

The school week was over, and I had just flown to Eli's house on my <u>hovercraft</u>. Eli stood at the entry portal, playing with his phone; he must have hit the "human <u>transport</u>" button, because he disappeared from the doorway and reappeared in the driveway, in front of me. He was holding his robot, W-52, who was a model from a few years ago. W-52 was moving a little slowly these days, but he still worked, so I was stunned when Eli dropped him into the garbage can as if he were trash.

"What are you doing?" I cried, "That's your pet!"

Eli laughed. "I'm getting a new, improved robot."

Down in the trash, W-52 rotated his arms slowly.

"But he looks miserable," I said. "We should repair him."

"What for, Hal?" Eli scoffed, "He's just a robot; quit acting like he has feelings."

I bit my lip to keep from saying anything more. Most people agree with Eli, that robots can't feel emotions, but I'd never believed that.

That night, I went back to Eli's and I retrieved W-52 from the trash, and though he was almost too weak to speak, he forced out one word: "Junkyard."

"What's at the junkyard?" I puzzled.

But before he could answer, W-52's eyes closed and he stopped moving. When I held my ear to him, I could hear a faint buzz, but I knew he didn't have much time left. The only thing to do was hop on my hovercraft and fly to the junkyard at speed 1000.

Reading Guide

What has been happening to the robots?

Where did the robots get their power from before? Where do they get it from now?

When we arrived, I couldn't believe my eyes; hundreds of robots were rolling around on their wheeled feet and climbing piles of car engines, fuel tanks, and rusted doors.

"W-52 is in trouble," I told them. "He instructed me to come here."

The robot at the top of the junk heap nodded. "Initiate climb-down," she ordered.

All the robots did as she requested, making it clear that she was their leader.

"My name is XR-20," she said. "Thank you for helping our friend."

"No thanks are necessary," I said. "But how can you help him here?"

As a team of robots rushed W-52 away, XR-20 explained the robots' current situation. She told me that the robots were originally solar powered and needed nothing but the sun's energy to keep them alive. But the solar squares that the robots had used to harness the sun's energy were cheaply made, and they soon ceased to function. Though it was possible to replace the squares, most people didn't bother, preferring to discard their old robots for newer models, just like Eli had.

"But what can you do about it here at the junkyard?" I asked.

"Most robots have the ability to use gas for fuel in case of solar square failure," XR-20 explained, "but sick robots rarely make it to the gas in time. I was fortunate in that my owner threw me away just as my solar square had started to fail; when I got to the junkyard, I had enough power to crawl to the nearest car and drink its fuel. The junkyard is full of old cars, you see, now that everyone drives a hovercraft."

XR-20 explained that she then started collecting ailing robots from people's garbage cans and bringing them to the junkyard, where she fed them fuel from the cars.

Why does Hal go see Professor Estrella?

How do Hal, Professor Estrella, and XR-20 work together? What is their goal?

"But now we robots face a new dilemma," XR-20 said, shaking her head sadly. "We are rapidly running out of gas."

That night, as I watched the robots work tirelessly to nurse W-52 back to health, I was sure of two things: robots *did* have feelings, and I had to help them.

The next morning, I typed *university* into my hovercraft's mapping system. There I met Professor Estrella, an expert on using the sun's energy. I explained the robots' situation.

The professor stared at the ceiling, deep in thought. "Robot owners need an easy, low-maintenance, low-cost solution. They need a reason to keep their old robots."

"Do you have any ideas?" I asked.

Professor Estrella nodded. "I've developed a new solar paint that has passed its endurance tests with flying colors. It's certified to last for at least a hundred years, and I have tons of it left over from testing."

The following week, Professor Estrella and I went to the junkyard and painted each robot with neon-yellow solar paint.

Our next step was spreading the word. With Professor Estrella's help, I opened a robot shelter right next door to the store where everyone buys new robots. Together the two of us worked to persuade people to adopt our repaired robots instead. Once people understood how long the solar paint lasted, they rushed to adopt their old robots back. I'm proud to say that as of today, there are no more robots at the junkyard; every single one has a forever home.

Answer the following questions.

1. How might the way the reader views robots be different if the passage were told from Eli's point of view?

   A. The reader would think that robots are a nuisance.

   B. The reader would think that robots should not be solar powered.

   C. The reader would think that robots are objects without feelings.

   D. The reader would think that robots can be dangerous.

2 Read the sentence in each choice on the left. Then match the underlined word in the sentence to its closest definition on the right.

A. The school week was over, and I had just flown to Eli's house on my <u>hovercraft</u>.

1. to get energy from the sun

2. to get energy from gas

B. Eli stood at the entry portal, playing with his phone; he must have hit the "human <u>transport</u>" button, because he disappeared from the doorway and reappeared in front of me.

3. to move something from one place to another

4. a robot that can speak and understand

C. She told me that the robots were originally <u>solar powered</u> and needed nothing but the sun's energy to keep them alive.

5. a vehicle that can fly or float in air

6. to get energy from a junkyard

3 The following question has two parts. First, answer Part A. Then, answer Part B.

Part A

Which of these sentences **best** states the conflict of the passage?

A. People want to adopt the old robots.

B. People are throwing away old robots.

C. Professor Estrella has invented solar paint.

D. Hal has to take W-52 to the junkyard.

Part B

Which sentence from the passage is the solution to the answer to Part A?

A. He was holding his robot, W-52, who was a model from a few years ago.

B. As a team of robots rushed W-52 away, XR-20 explained the robots' current situation.

C. The next morning, I typed *university* into my hovercraft's mapping system.

D. Together the two of us worked to persuade people to adopt our repaired robots instead.

4 Which of the following sentences from the passage is a clue that the passage is science fiction? Choose **all** that apply.

A. Eli stood at the entry portal, playing with his phone; he must have hit the "human transport" button, because he disappeared from the doorway and reappeared in front of me.

B. The only thing to do was hop on my hovercraft and fly to the junkyard at speed 1000.

C. As a team of robots rushed W-52 away, XR-20 explained the robots' current situation.

D. There I met Professor Estrella, an expert on using the sun's energy.

E. The professor stared at the ceiling, deep in thought.

5 The following question has two parts. First, answer Part A. Then, answer Part B.

Part A

Circle the statement about the characters that is supported by evidence in the passage.

Eli is full of big ideas. Hal doesn't like to think about the future.
Eli is impatient and a bit thoughtless. Hal is more questioning.
Eli likes a challenge. Hal wants life to be easy.

Part B

Write **two** details from the passage, one about Eli and one about Hal, to support the answer to Part A.

_____

_____

_____

_____

6 Compare and contrast the settings of "Operation Robot Rescue" and "A Birthday Brainstorm." Explain how each setting affects the plot of the passage. What types of events can happen in the setting the author chose? Use details from the passages to support your response.

Write your answer on the lines below.

_____

_____

_____

_____

_____

_____

_____

_____

_____

_____

_____

_____

_____

_____

RL.5.2, RL.5.4, RL.5.5, RL.5.6, L.5.4.a, L.5.5.a

Poetry

❶ GETTING THE IDEA

Poetry is a type of writing in which the poet uses descriptive language and sound devices, such as rhythm and rhyme, to create meaning and produce emotion in readers.

It often takes multiple readings to completely understand a poem. During the first reading, think about the poem's topic and the images it creates. During other readings, think about the poem's structure, poetic devices, and figurative language.

Structure

You can often recognize poetry by its structure. Poetry is usually made up of **lines**, which are rows of text. Lines may or may not be complete sentences. In a poem, lines are often grouped into sections called **stanzas**. Poets often develop their ideas by having stanzas build on one another.

Rhythm

Most poems have rhythm, which makes them fun to listen to and read aloud. **Rhythm** is the pattern of stressed and unstressed syllables in a line. Say the word *poet* aloud. You can hear that the first syllable is stressed, or said more strongly, and the second syllable is unstressed: *PO-et*.

Read aloud the following poem. Pay attention to which syllables you stress as you read.

> ### There Was an Old Man with a Nose
> *by Edward Lear*
>
> There was an Old Man with a nose,
> Who said, 'If you choose to suppose,
> That my nose is too long,
> You are certainly wrong!'
> That remarkable Man with a nose.

Rhyme

Many poems have lines that end with words that **rhyme**, or have the same ending sounds. When that is the case, the poem has a **rhyme scheme**, or rhyme pattern. You can show the rhyme scheme by giving each new sound at the end of a line a new letter. Read aloud the following rhyme. Write the letters *a* and *b* next to each line below to show the rhyme scheme.

> Pease porridge hot,
> Pease porridge cold.
> Pease porridge in the pot
> Nine days old.

Repetition

In poetry, **repetition** is the use of the same sounds, words, or lines. Poets often use repetition to help unify a poem or to reinforce the meaning or theme. Read the following poem. Circle the words that are repeated.

Two Birds and Their Nest
by Walt Whitman

> Two guests from Alabama—two together,
> And their nest, and four light-green eggs,
>   spotted with brown,
> And every day the he-bird, to and fro, near at hand,
> And every day the she-bird, crouch'd on her nest,
> And every day I, a curious boy, never too close,
>   never disturbing them,
> Cautiously peering.

Alliteration is the repetition of an initial consonant sound. Most tongue twisters use alliteration. Read the following sentence. Circle the initial consonant whose sound is repeated.

> Peter Piper picked a peck of pickled peppers.

Figurative Language

Poets use **figurative language** to create images with words. Two kinds of figurative language are similes and metaphors.

- A **simile** is a comparison of two unlike things or ideas that uses the word *like* or the word *as*.
- A **metaphor** is a comparison that does not use the word *like* or the word *as*. It says that one thing *is* another thing.

Read the following sentence. Is it a simile or a metaphor? What is being compared?

Joe is a big, cranky baby when he doesn't get his way.

Point of View and Theme

Point of view is the position or outlook from which the speaker tells a story or observes something. The **speaker** in a poem tells the poem, much like the narrator of a story tells the story. The speaker is the voice of the poem and can represent the poet or another person or character. Poets may write poems from different points of view.

- **First-person point of view** reveals the speaker's thoughts. The speaker directly observes or experiences what the poem describes. This point of view uses first-person pronouns.

- **Third-person point of view** reveals the thoughts and observations of someone who is *not* directly involved in the poem. This point of view does not use first-person pronouns.

The **theme** is the central idea a poem explores. Read the following poem. Circle the line that first reveals the poem's point of view. Then explain the poem's theme.

I'm Nobody! Who Are You?

by Emily Dickinson

I'm nobody! Who are you?
Are you nobody, too?
Then there's a pair of us—don't tell!
They'd banish us, you know.

How dreary to be somebody!
How public, like a frog
To tell your name the livelong day
To an admiring bog!

Kinds of Poetry

There are many kinds of poems. The chart below defines some of them.

Kind of Poem	Definition
lyric poem	a short poem that is like a song and usually deals with personal feelings and states of mind
epic poem	a long poem that tells about the adventures of a hero or a historic event
sonnet	a poem that has fourteen lines with ten to twelve syllables per line and a rhyme scheme
ballad	a poem that tells a story with short stanzas containing an equal number of lines and a refrain that repeats
light verse	a poem that is humorous and often silly; light verse is usually short and uses clever word play
free verse	a poem that does not follow any fixed rules of rhythm or rhyme or traditional structure

Language Spotlight • Antiquated Language

When you read older poems, you will often come across **antiquated**, or old-fashioned, language. Some antiquated words are old forms of words we still use, such as *thou* for *you*. Others are words that we no longer use frequently, if at all. You can often use context to figure out the meaning of an antiquated word. However, sometimes you may have to look up the word in a dictionary.

Read the following poem. Write the modern word for each underlined word. Use a dictionary if you need to.

from Written in March
by William Wordsworth

Like an army defeated
The snow <u>hath</u> retreated,
And now <u>doth</u> fare ill
On top of the bare hill;
The <u>ploughboy</u> is whooping—anon—anon

Read the poem.

Pop-Corn

from Child Songs of Cheer
by Evaleen Stein

> *Pop! Pop!—Poppetty-pop!*
> Shake and rattle and rattle and shake
> The golden grains as they bounce and break
> To fluffy puffiness—*Poppetty-pop!*
> 5 Bursting and banging the popper's top!
> *Poppetty-pop!*
> *Pop! Pop!*
> The yellow kernels, oh, see them grow
> White as cotton or flakes of snow!
> 10 *Pop! Pop!*
> O-ho, how they frolic and fly about
> And turn themselves suddenly inside out!
> *Pop-pop-poppetty! Pop-pop-pop!*
> The popper's full and we'll have to stop;
> 15 Pile the bowl with the tempting treat,
> Children, come, it is time to eat!

Answer the following questions.

1 Read this line from the poem.

White as cotton or flakes of snow!

Which of the following does the line include? Choose **all** that apply.

A. alliteration

B. metaphor

C. repetition

D. rhyme

E. rhythm

F. simile

> **Hint** Think about what each of these poetic terms means. Then say the line aloud. What are some sounds of poetry? What creates an image in your mind?

2 Read the following lines from the poem. Write *a* or *b* in each box to show the rhyme scheme.

☐ *Pop-pop-poppetty! Pop-pop-pop!*

☐ The popper's full and we'll have to stop;

☐ Pile the bowl with the tempting treat,

☐ Children, come, it is time to eat!

> **Hint** Remember to use the same letter for two or more lines that rhyme with each other.

3 How does the poet use repetition in the poem? What effect does the repetition have? Write your answer on the lines below.

_____

_____

_____

_____

> **Hint** Look for words and phrases that the poet uses over and over again. Then read the poem aloud and picture what is being described to help you determine the effect of the repetition.

4 The following question has two parts. First, answer Part A. Then, answer Part B.

Part A

From whose point of view is "Pop-Corn" told?

A. a speaker not involved in the action

B. a speaker who wants to be in the action

C. a speaker who ignores the action

D. a speaker taking part in the action

Part B

Circle the line in the poem that supports the answer to Part A.

> **Hint** Think about who the speaker is in the poem. What kinds of pronouns does the speaker use?

Use the Reading Guide to help you understand the poem.

Father William

from Alice's Adventures in Wonderland
by Lewis Carroll

Reading Guide

Which words rhyme? What is the rhyme scheme?

What are Father William's reasons for the things he does?

Who is the speaker in each stanza? How does the organization of the stanzas help you understand the poem?

"You are old, Father William," the young man said,
  "And your hair has become very white;
And yet you incessantly stand on your head—
  Do you think, at your age, it is right?"

5 "In my youth," Father William replied to his son,
  "I feared it might injure the brain;
But, now that I'm perfectly sure I have none,
  Why, I do it again and again."

"You are old," said the youth, "as I mentioned before,
10 And have grown most uncommonly fat;
Yet you turned a back-somersault in at the door—
  Pray, what is the reason of that?"

"In my youth," said the sage, as he shook his grey locks,
  "I kept all my limbs very supple
15 By the use of this ointment—one shilling the box—
  Allow me to sell you a couple?"

"You are old," said the youth, "and your jaws are too weak
  For anything tougher than suet;
Yet you finished the goose, with the bones and the beak—
20 Pray how did you manage to do it?"

"In my youth," said his father, "I took to the law,
  And argued each case with my wife;
And the muscular strength, which it gave to my jaw,
  Has lasted the rest of my life."

How does the poet use repetition?

What is the last thing Father William says to his son? Why?

25 "You are old," said the youth, "one would hardly suppose
    That your eye was as steady as ever;
Yet you balanced an eel on the end of your nose—
    What made you so awfully clever?"

"I have answered three questions, and that is enough,"
30   Said his father; "don't give yourself airs!
Do you think I can listen all day to such stuff?
    Be off, or I'll kick you down stairs!"

Answer the following questions.

1 This question has two parts. First, answer Part A. Then, answer Part B.

Part A

Which **best** describes the theme of the poem?

  A. Older people should act their age.

  B. Younger people should respect their elders.

  C. Older people should teach younger people.

  D. Younger people should learn from older people.

Part B

Circle the lines in the poem that support the answer to Part A.

2 Read the following lines from the poem. Write *a* or *b* in each box to show the rhyme scheme.

☐	"You are old," said the youth, "and your jaws are too weak
☐	For anything tougher than suet;
☐	Yet you finished the goose, with the bones and the beak—
☐	Pray how did you manage to do it?"

3 Read the following lines from the poem.

"I have answered three questions, and that is enough,"

Said his father; "don't give yourself airs!"

What is the meaning of airs as it is used in the poem?

A. tunes

B. a surrounding influence

C. an attitude of being better than everyone else

D. a mixture of gases that surround Earth

4 Which sentence **best** explains why Lewis Carroll probably wrote this poem? Choose **all** that apply.

A. He wanted to use words to create an image of the son.

B. He wanted to please and amuse his readers.

C. He wanted to show what it is like to be old.

D. He wanted to make his readers feel sorry for Father William.

E. He wanted to create a ridiculous character.

F. He wanted to tell a moving story about a father and a son.

5 The following question has two parts. First, answer Part A. Then, answer Part B.

Part A

Which word **best** describes Father William? Choose **all** that apply.

A. anxious

B. cautious

C. confused

D. fearless

E. impatient

F. uncertain

Part B

Underline **two** lines in the poem that support the answer to Part A.

6 From whose point of view is "Father William" told?

A. Father William

B. the youth

C. a speaker taking part in the action

D. a speaker not involved in the action

7 The poet organizes the poem into eight stanzas of four lines each. Explain why the poet **most likely** organizes the poem in this way. How does the poem's structure affect the narrative? How does it affect the humor? Support your answer with details from the poem.

Write your answer on the lines below.

_____

_____

_____

_____

_____

_____

_____

_____

_____

_____

_____

_____

_____

_____

_____

Drama

① GETTING THE IDEA

A **drama** is a story meant to be performed by actors. Movies, television shows, and plays are dramas. Like other types of fiction, dramas have a setting, characters, a plot, and a theme.

The first thing you might notice about a drama is that it looks different from a novel or short story. The key to understanding a drama is to understand the elements that make up a drama and how those elements work together.

Element	Definition
act	a main section of a drama's action
scene	a section of an act
cast of characters	the characters in a drama
setting	the place and time where the action takes place
dialogue	the words spoken by a character
stage direction	an action that is performed by a character

Act and Scene

A drama is made up of one or more **acts**, or sections, that are often divided into smaller sections called **scenes**. There is often a new act or scene when there is a change in the setting or main action, or when a different group of characters enters the action.

Cast of Characters

The **cast of characters** appears at the beginning of a drama and lists all the characters in the drama. Characters may be listed in the order in which they appear in the play or in order of importance. Sometimes, a character's name is followed by a brief description.

Setting

In a drama, the **setting** is described at the beginning of the play and at the beginning of each scene. It is usually in italic type and tells when and where the action takes place. The location in which a play is set, and how it is described, often affects what the characters say and do. Read the following setting and underline the words that tell where and when the drama takes place. What kind of characters might you expect to see in this setting? What might the story be about?

Late at night, a plain, tidy cottage in a clearing in the woods. A milking stool and an overturned bucket are by the front door.

Dialogue

Dialogue is made up of the words characters say. Most of the story in a drama is told through dialogue. Dialogue appears after a character's name and is not set within quotation marks. You can make inferences about the characters based on what they say and do, how they respond to others, and how other characters respond to them.

Underline the dialogue in the excerpt below. What can you infer about Jack and Mother from the dialogue?

JACK: Mother! I traded our cow for these magic beans.
MOTHER: Magic beans! What good are they? What we need is food!

Stage Directions

Stage directions tell characters how to act or speak their lines. They also tell more about the setting, characters, and plot with information about sound, lighting, props, and costumes. Stage directions are often printed in italics inside parentheses.

Read the following stage directions. What do they tell you about the setting, the props, and the character's actions?

(*Low lights to show dawn. Birds sing. Jack exits cottage, yawning and holding a bucket. Suddenly, he sees a towering beanstalk where Mother threw the magic beans. He stares, mouth open wide.*)

Putting It All Together

When you read a drama, pay attention to all of its parts. Use details in the dialogue and stage directions to make inferences about the characters. Think about how the setting affects what the characters say and do. Use context clues to figure out the meaning of unknown words and antiquated, or old-fashioned, language.

Read the excerpt below. Then answer the questions.

> (*Jack grabs the bag of gold coins, hears pounding footsteps, hides under the table. Giant enters.*)
> GIANT: (*booms*) Servant, bring me my dinner! Food! I want food!
> (*Servant enters with a bowl of food. Giant eats greedily, belches, then falls asleep with his face in his bowl, snoring. Jack emerges.*)
> JACK: (*whispers to audience*) Hark! He sleeps. I'll grab the gold coins and flee!

- How do sounds in the stage directions affect Jack's actions?
- How would you describe Giant? Cite evidence from the text.
- What does the word *hark* mean? What clues help you know?

Language Spotlight • Figurative Language

Dramas, like other works of fiction, sometimes use figurative language to express an idea in a new way. **Figurative language** is language that goes beyond the literal meaning of the words to create an image in the reader's mind. Here are some examples.

- An **idiom** is a common phrase whose words mean something entirely different from the individual words, such as *give me a hand*.
- A **proverb** is a common saying that expresses advice based on experience, such as *the squeaky wheel gets the grease*.
- An **adage** is a saying that expresses an accepted truth about life. For example, *practice makes perfect*.
- An **allusion** uses a well-known person, place, or event in history or literature to make a comparison. What comparison is the father making in this example? What is he implying? A father speaking to his son: "Be careful, Pinocchio, your nose is growing."

Read the play.

A Little More Salt

Cast of Characters

DAD
MOM
DAUGHTER
SON

Act I, Scene 1

Early evening. A modern kitchen. Table is set for dinner. Dad is stirring the stew he is making for dinner. Dad is tasting the stew when the rest of the family enters.

MOM: Hello, dear. Did you have a good day? Oh, stew! Can I have a taste?

DAD: Certainly. It's almost ready. I'm just looking for . . . (*Dad squats to look through one of the lower cabinets. Mom lifts the ladle to her lips and frowns.*)

DAUGHTER: (*holding cell phone against chest*) I want a taste, too, Dad! (*resuming phone conversation*) Yeah, I know. Can you believe it? And then he . . . I know, I know.

SON: Stew! My favorite! I'm so hungry I could eat a horse. (*opens mouth*)

(*Mom gives daughter and son a taste. Both frown.*)

DAUGHTER: (*still frowning*) Something's missing. (*resuming phone conversation*) No, sorry, not talking to you. Sorry. No, I know. Absolutely. I don't know what she sees in him; he's no Romeo! We should say something. After all, honesty is the best policy.

DAD: Now where did I . . . ? (*begins searching the pantry*) Ten more minutes everyone. Go wash up.

(*Daughter exits, still on cell phone. Son exits, leaving guitar behind.*)

MOM: I think it needs a little salt, dear.

(*Dad nods, rummaging through the pantry. Mom sees a saltshaker on the table, grabs it, and adds salt to the stew. She places the shaker on the counter by the stove and exits.*)

Act I, Scene 2

DAD: Where is that salt? (*turns, sees saltshaker, palm slaps forehead*) There it is! I was beginning to think it had walked away. (*adds salt to stew and stirs, then adds a little more*) Five more minutes!

(*Dad exits.*)

(*Son enters, grabs guitar, and sees saltshaker.*)

SON: A shake or two is all it needs. (*adds salt and exits with guitar*)

(*Daughter enters, sees saltshaker.*)

DAUGHTER: A little salt should do the trick. (*adds salt, sits at the table*)

(*Mom and Son enter and sit. Dad carries over the stew and sits.*)

MOM: Looks good, dear!

DAUGHTER: Yeah, Dad. It smells good, too!

SON: Mmmmm . . .

(*Dad ladles out the stew into each person's bowl.*)

DAD: OK, everyone! Dig in!

(*Everyone takes a mouthful of stew. An expression of distaste appears on each face.*)

DAD: (*grimacing*) I only added a little salt.

MOM: Oh, my! So did I!

DAUGHTER and SON: (*in unison*) So did I!

(*All characters laugh. Light fades. Curtain falls.*)

Answer the following questions.

1 Read this excerpt from the play.

We should say something. After all, honesty is the best policy.

Explain the figurative language in the excerpt.

_____

_____

_____

> **Hint** Look back at the different types of figurative language to help you determine the type of saying used in the excerpt.

2 The following question has two parts. First, answer Part A. Then, answer Part B.

Part A

What does the phrase <u>dig in</u> mean as it is used in the play?

A. dig food out of a pot

B. divide food into portions

C. to enjoy your food

D. start eating your food

Part B

Which stage directions helped you figure out the answer to Part A?

A. _Dad carries over the stew and sits._

B. _Dad ladles out the stew into each person's bowl._

C. _Everyone takes a mouthful of stew._

D. _An expression of distaste appears on each face._

> **Hint** Go back to the play. Look at the words and lines around the phrase _dig in_. How do the characters' actions help you understand the phrase?

3 Consider why the author includes two scenes. Tell how the scenes work together to develop the plot and give structure to the play.

Write your answers on the lines provided.

_____

_____

_____

_____

Hint Remember that a new scene often indicates a change in the setting, the plot, or a group of characters.

4 The following question has two parts. First, answer Part A. Then, answer Part B.

Part A

Which of the following **best** states the theme of "A Little More Salt"?

A. A watched pot never boils.

B. Too many cooks spoil the broth.

C. Appearances can be deceiving.

D. If you can't take the heat, get out of the kitchen.

Part B

Explain how the events in the play support the answer to Part A.

Hint The theme is the message that the author wants readers to take away from a story. Think about the life lesson this drama shares.

Use the Reading Guide to help you understand the play.

excerpted from

Each in His Own Place

by Augusta Stevenson

Reading Guide

What does the cast of characters tell you about the characters?

Why is Sausage so upset at the beginning of the play?

Cast of Characters:

SAUSAGE, who stirs the pot
COAL, who makes the fire
SUGAR LOAF,[1] who lays the table
STRAW, who brings in the wood
SNOWFLAKE, who draws the water
DOG, who waits

Act I, Scene 1

Yesterday, in a tiny house. The tiny kitchen is seen. The Sausage is stirring the pot. The Coal is tending the fire. The Sugar Loaf is laying the table. Enter Straw with a load of wood.

STRAW: (*throwing down wood*) Think you'll need more wood for the dinner, Sausage?

(*Sausage does not answer. She gets into the pot to flavor the vegetables.*)

COAL: (*whispers to Straw*) Sausage is quite put out.

STRAW: What's the trouble?

COAL: No one knows.

(*Enter Snowflake with a pail of water. . . . Sausage comes out of the pot.*)

SNOWFLAKE: Here is the water, Sausage.

(*Sausage does not answer.*)

[1] **sugar loaf:** a tall cone of sugar; This is how sugar was prepared before there were sugar cubes or granulated sugar.

Consider each character's reason for not changing jobs. How are their excuses valid?

What is the purpose of drawing the paper slips?

SNOWFLAKE: (*speaking louder*) Will you come for the water, Sausage?

SAUSAGE: (*sharply*) No, madam, I will not! . . . I've been slave here long enough! . . .

SNOWFLAKE: Have I not done my share of the work?

COAL: Have I not done my share?

STRAW: Have I not done my share?

SUGAR LOAF: And have I not done my share?

SAUSAGE: Please tell me what you do.

STRAW: I bring in wood that Coal may make the fire.

COAL: I make the fire that the pot may boil.

SNOWFLAKE: I draw the water and bring it from the brook.

SUGAR LOAF: I lay the table nicely.

SAUSAGE: What do I? Eh? What do I? I must stand over the fire. I must not only stir the dinner, I must flavor it with myself. For each of you there is one duty. For me there are plainly three. . . . There must be a change! Someone else can stand over the fire—can stir the pot—can flavor the vegetables.

COAL: If I flavored them, they could not be eaten.

SAUSAGE: That's what you're always saying, but I'm not so sure of it.

SNOWFLAKE: If I stirred the pot, 't would be the end of me.

SAUSAGE: Yes, you say that often enough, but I'm not so sure that it is true.

STRAW: Should I stand over the fire, I'd be no more.

SAUSAGE: (*scornfully*) Excuses! Excuses!

SUGAR LOAF: 'T is plain that I should not get into the pot.

SAUSAGE: And why not, Miss? Why not?

Reading Guide

SUGAR LOAF: 'T would be good-by for me, if I should!

SAUSAGE: Excuses! Excuses! I say there must be a change! 'T is I who will bring the wood or draw the water.

COAL: But, Sausage, you should stay within.

SAUSAGE: Not I, sir! I'll out of the pot and out of the house, I will! I'll see a bit of the world, I will! . . . (*gets slips of paper*) Come, now, and draw for it. (*She holds the slips for the others to draw.*)

STRAW: (*drawing; reading from slip*) "Who gets this must make the fire."

SUGAR LOAF: (*drawing; reading from slip*) "Who gets this must draw the water."

SNOWFLAKE: (*drawing; reading from slip*) "Who gets this must stir the pot and flavor it with herself."

COAL: (*drawing; reading from slip*) "Who gets this must lay the table nicely."

SAUSAGE: (*reading from last slip*) "Who gets this must bring the wood." Well, that pleases me! Straw, see if the fire needs wood. (*Straw hesitates.*) Come, come, do your duty!

(*Straw crosses the hearth and looks into the fire. He is very careful, but the fire reaches him and he is gone in a puff!*)

SNOWFLAKE: Poor Straw! Well, 't is my duty to stir the pot and to flavor it with myself.

(*She crosses to the hearth, but just as she reaches it, she disappears without so much as a cry.*)

SUGAR LOAF: Poor Snowflake! Well, 't is my duty to draw the water.

(*She forgets that the pail is full, falls into it, and is seen no more.*)

COAL: Poor Sugar Loaf! Well, 't is my duty to lay the table nicely.

Sausage says, "They always said my place was within." What does Sausage means by this?

What does Dog mean when he says "I'll put you there" to Sausage?

(*He forgets that he is still burning from having lately tended the fire. As he places the plates, the tablecloth catches fire and wraps itself around him.*)

COAL: (*from inside the burning cloth*) This is the end of me!

SAUSAGE: (*weeping*) Dear me! Dear me! Who would have thought 't would turn out so badly! Well, 't is my duty to bring in wood.

(*She opens the door and is face to face with a hungry dog who is sniffing about.*)

DOG: Ah, I thought you'd be coming out soon! . . .

SAUSAGE: How good to be out in the world! They always said my place was within.

DOG: They did, eh? Well, just to please them, I'll put you there.

(*He swallows her quickly, which ends both Sausage and our story.*)

Answer the following questions.

1 In what ways are Snowflake and Sugar Loaf alike? Choose **all** that apply.

A. They both feel they do their share of the work.

B. They both understand that Sausage has the most important job.

C. They both believe that stirring the pot would be the end of them.

D. They both approach their new jobs without complaint.

2 Read the following excerpt from the play.

SAUSAGE: For each of you there is one duty. For me there is plainly three. . . . There must be a change!

How does Sausage's demand create a problem for the other characters? How do the characters attempt to address this problem?

Write your answer on the lines below.

_____

_____

_____

_____

3 Which proverb **best** relates to the lesson that can be learned from Sausage's actions?

A. The early bird catches the worm.

B. People who live in glass houses should not throw stones.

C. Good things come to those who wait.

D. Be careful what you wish for.

4 The following question has two parts. First, answer Part A. Then, answer Part B.

Part A

Circle the statement that is supported by evidence in the play.

Sausage is selfish. Coal is thoughtful of others.
Sausage is impatient and takes risks. Coal is happy with his life.
Sausage wants things to stay as they are. Coal wants a change.

Part B

Write **two** details from the play, one about Sausage and one about Coal, that support the answer to Part A.

_____

_____

_____

5 Think about what the characters do and say in the beginning, middle, and end of the play. How do the characters' words and actions move the plot forward?

_____

_____

_____

_____

_____

_____

_____

_____

6 The title of this drama is *Each in His Own Place*. How does the title relate to the theme of the play? Think about what Sausage wants and what happens when she accomplishes her goal. Use details from the play to support your response.

Write your answer on the lines below.

_____

_____

_____

_____

_____

_____

_____

_____

_____

_____

_____

_____

_____

_____

_____

RL.5.2, RL.5.3, RL.5.9, L.5.4, L.5.4.a

Analyze Literature

1 GETTING THE IDEA

Readers are always making connections between what they are reading and what they've read in the past. A story about a family moving to a new planet might make you think of a story about a family moving westward in the 1800s. Characters, setting, plot, theme, and author's style can be compared and contrasted across types of literature. When you **compare**, you tell how things are similar. When you **contrast**, you tell how they are different.

Compare and Contrast Characters

Characters in different types of fiction may have a lot in common. Or, two characters in stories about the same topic may be very different. To examine characters:

- Look for physical descriptions of the characters. How do the characters look?

- Look at what the characters say and do. What do their words and actions tell you about their personalities?

The following passages are from different stories. How are James and Will alike? How are they different?

James stared at the floor, walking hesitantly into his new school. As other kids rushed past, James wished he could become invisible. Even after moving so many times, starting at a new school never got easier. He hoped he would make new friends.

Another year, another school. Will was used to it by now. He strode confidently through the doors of his new school, smiling at everyone who looked his way. He was thrilled by all the new faces; there was nothing he liked more than making new friends and exploring a new place.

Compare and Contrast Settings

Two stories may be set in the same place at different times in history, or in two different places at the same time in history. Even if two stories are set in the exact same place *and* time, their subjects may be different. To examine settings:

- Look for details about the surroundings. What does the land look like? What is the weather? What kinds of buildings are there?

- Look for details about the people. How do the characters dress and speak?

Compare and Contrast Plot

When comparing and contrasting plots, look for details about the characters' conflicts and how they resolve those conflicts.

Compare and Contrast Theme

Two stories might have the same theme—such as overcoming fear—but the main characters may overcome their fears in different ways. Read the following passages. How are the characters, settings, and plots similar? How are they different? What theme do the passages share?

Lauren spotted something on the sidewalk outside a store. It was a wallet full of money. She looked around. No one had seen her pick it up. She thought about the things she could buy with that money, but her heart felt heavy. *I might buy nice things, but I wouldn't enjoy them*, she thought. She walked into the store and asked to speak to the manager. Maybe someone had reported a missing wallet.

A poor woodcutter accidentally dropped his old axe into the river. He began to cry, for without his axe, he had no way to work. Suddenly, Mercury, god of the sea, swam up holding a golden axe. "Is this yours?" Mercury asked. "No," said the woodcutter. "My ax is old and rusted." Mercury said, "You are an honest man. Take this golden ax as a reward for telling the truth."

Compare and Contrast Author's Style

Every author has a unique **style**. An author's style is made up of his or her word choice, language, and sentence structure. Notice whether the author uses formal or informal language, and whether the author uses short, simple sentences or longer sentences full of description and figurative language.

Style may affect how a reader reacts to a story. For example, a reader who prefers serious stories over humorous ones will likely enjoy a serious story more. And some readers may not enjoy stories with a lot of old-fashioned language.

Comparing and Contrasting Checklist

These questions can help you compare and contrast stories:

- What is the main character like?
- How does the main character react to situations and other characters?
- What is the setting?
- What are the plot events?
- What is the theme?
- What kind of style does the author use?

Language Spotlight • Multiple-Meaning Words

Multiple-meaning words are words that have more than one meaning. The different meanings may even be different parts of speech. Using context clues can help you figure out which meaning is intended. Read the definitions and sentences below. Circle the context clues that help you determine the meaning of *present* in each sentence.

present as a verb meaning "to give"	Today, Matt's principal was planning to present him with an art award.
present as an adjective meaning "in a place"	But when Matt's teacher took attendance, Matt wasn't present. He was home sick.
present as a noun meaning "a gift"	After school, Matt's teacher brought him a present. Matt unwrapped it and found the award!

Read the passage.

excerpted from

How the Rhinoceros Got His Skin

by Rudyard Kipling

Once upon a time, on an uninhabited island on the shores of the Red Sea, there lived a Parsee.[1] . . . And the Parsee lived by the Red Sea with nothing but his hat and his knife and a cooking-stove. . . . One day he took flour and water and currants and plums and sugar and things, and made himself one cake. . . . But just as he was going to eat it there came down to the beach . . . one Rhinoceros with a horn on his nose, two piggy eyes, and few manners. In those days the Rhinoceros's skin fitted him quite tight. There were no wrinkles in it anywhere. . . . The Parsee left that cake and climbed to the top of a palm. . . . And the Rhinoceros . . . spiked that cake on the horn of his nose, and he ate it, and he went away, waving his tail. . . . Then the Parsee came down from his palm-tree and put the stove on its legs and recited the following . . .

> *Them that takes cakes*
> *Which the Parsee-man bakes*
> *Makes dreadful mistakes. . . .*

Because, five weeks later, there was a heat wave in the Red Sea. . . . The Rhinoceros took off his skin and carried it over his shoulder as he came down to the beach to bathe. In those days it buttoned underneath with three buttons. . . . He waddled straight into the water and blew bubbles through his nose, leaving his skin on the beach.

Presently the Parsee came by and found the skin, and he smiled one smile that ran all round his face two times. . . . Then he went to his camp and filled his hat with cake-crumbs. . . . He took that skin, and he shook that skin, and he scrubbed that skin, and he rubbed that skin just as full of old, dry, stale, tickly cake-crumbs and some burned currants as ever it could possibly hold. Then he climbed to the top of his palm-tree and waited for the Rhinoceros to come out of the water. . . .

[1] **Parsee**: an old-fashioned word meaning "someone from Persia"

And the Rhinoceros did. He buttoned it up with the three buttons, and it tickled like cake crumbs in bed. Then he wanted to scratch, but that made it worse. . . Then he lay down on the sands and rolled and rolled. . . . Then he ran to the palm-tree and rubbed and rubbed. . . . He rubbed so much and so hard that he rubbed his skin into a great fold over his shoulders, and another fold underneath, where the buttons used to be. . . . But it didn't make the least difference to the cake-crumbs. . . . So he went home, very angry indeed and horribly scratchy. . . . From that day to this every rhinoceros has great folds in his skin and a very bad temper. . . .

Answer the following questions.

1 Which word **best** describes the Parsee?

   A. calm

   B. generous

   C. greedy

   D. unforgiving

> **Hint** Think about what the Parsee does and why he does it. What word best fits his actions?

2 Which of the following **best** describes the author's language style? Choose **all** that apply.

   A. serious

   B. playful

   C. old-fashioned

   D. funny

   E. stiff

   F. modern

> **Hint** Does the passage sound like something that was written today or long ago? How is the language meant to make readers feel?

3 The following question has two parts. First, answer Part A. Then, answer Part B.

Part A

Which **best** states the theme of the passage?

A. Politeness is a virtue.

B. Bad behavior has consequences.

C. Revenge is never right.

D. It's best to plan ahead.

Part B

Which excerpt from the passage supports the answer to Part A?

A. One day he took flour and water and currants and plums and sugar and things, and made himself one cake.

B. In those days the Rhinoceros's skin fitted him quite tight.

C. And the Rhinoceros . . . spiked that cake on the horn of his nose, and he ate it, and he went away, waving his tail.

D. *Them that takes cakes / Which the Parsee-man bakes / Makes dreadful mistakes.*

Hint To figure out a theme, think about what happens to the characters and how they change. What happens to Rhinoceros in this passage?

4 Read the following excerpt from the passage.

And the Rhinoceros . . . spiked that cake on the horn of his nose, and he ate it, and he went away, waving his tail.

Based on this excerpt, what can you tell about the Rhinoceros's character?

_____

_____

_____

Hint Does the cake belong to the Rhinoceros? Does he have permission to take it?

Use the Reading Guide to help you understand the passage.

excerpted from

How the Whale Got His Throat

by Rudyard Kipling

Reading Guide

What does the Whale eat at the beginning of the story?

Is the narrator a character from the story or someone outside of the action?

Why does the Whale decide to eat Man?

In the sea, once upon a time, . . . there was a Whale, and he ate fishes. . . . All the fishes he could find in all the sea he ate with his mouth—so! Till at last there was only one small fish left in all the sea, and he was a small 'Stute Fish.
. . . He swam a little behind the Whale's right ear, so as to be out of harm's way. Then the Whale stood up on his tail and said, "I'm hungry." And the small 'Stute Fish said in a small 'stute voice, ". . . Have you ever tasted Man?"

"No," said the Whale. "What is it like?"

"Nice," said the small 'Stute Fish. "Nice but nubbly."

"Then fetch me some," said the Whale, and he made the sea froth up with his tail.

"One at a time is enough," said the 'Stute Fish. "If you swim to latitude[1] Fifty North, longitude[1] Forty West, . . . you will find, sitting *on* a raft, *in* the middle of the sea, with nothing on but a pair of blue canvas breeches, a pair of suspenders, . . . and a jack-knife, one ship-wrecked Mariner.[2] . . ."

So the Whale swam and swam to latitude Fifty North, longitude Forty West, as fast as he could swim. And *on* a raft, *in* the middle of the sea, *with* nothing to wear except a pair of blue canvas breeches, a pair of suspenders, . . . *and* a jack-knife, he found one single, solitary shipwrecked Mariner. . . .

[1] **latitude, longitude**: imaginary lines around Earth that can be used to find a specific location

[2] **mariner**: a sailor

Reading Guide

What does the Whale swallow with the Mariner?

What kind of language does the author use in this passage?

Where does the Mariner want to go?

Then the Whale opened his mouth back and back and back till it nearly touched his tail. . . . And he swallowed the shipwrecked Mariner, and the raft he was sitting on, and his blue canvas breeches, and the suspenders, . . . *and* the jack-knife. He swallowed them all down into his warm, dark, inside cup-boards, and then he smacked his lips. . . .

But as soon as the Mariner . . . found himself truly inside the Whale's warm, dark, inside cup-boards, he stumped and he jumped and he thumped and he bumped. . . . And he pranced and he danced, and he banged and he clanged. . . . And the Whale felt most unhappy indeed. . . .

So he said to the 'Stute Fish, "This man is very nubbly, and besides he is making me hiccough. What shall I do?"

"Tell him to come out," said the 'Stute Fish.

So the Whale called down his own throat to the shipwrecked Mariner, "Come out and behave yourself. I've got the hiccoughs."

"Nay, nay!" said the Mariner. "Not so, but far otherwise. Take me to my natal[3]-shore and the white-cliffs-of-Albion, and I'll think about it." And he began to dance more than ever.

"You had better take him home," said the 'Stute Fish to the Whale. . . .

So the Whale swam and swam and swam, with both flippers and his tail, as hard as he could. . . . At last he saw the Mariner's natal-shore and the white-cliffs-of-Albion, . . .

[3] **natal**: the place where someone is born; "The white-cliffs-of-Albion" refers to the seacoast town of Dover, England.

What does the Mariner do to the Whale? How does he stop the Whale from eating?

Why does the Whale now eat only very small fish?

He rushed half-way up the beach, and opened his mouth wide and wide and wide, and said, "Change here for . . . stations on the Fitchburg Road."[4] And just as he said 'Fitch' the Mariner walked out of his mouth. But while the Whale had been swimming, the Mariner . . . had taken his jack-knife and cut up the raft into a little square grating all running criss-cross, and he had tied it firm with his suspenders. . . . And he dragged that grating good and tight into the Whale's throat, and there it stuck! Then he recited the following . . .

By means of a grating
I have stopped your ating.[5]

For the Mariner . . . he married and lived happily ever afterward. So did the Whale. But from that day on, the grating in his throat, which he could neither cough up nor swallow down, prevented him eating anything except very, very small fish. And that is the reason why whales nowadays never eat men or boys or little girls.

[4] The Whale is speaking like a train conductor, calling out stops on the train.

[5] **ating**: eating

Answer the following questions about both passages in this lesson.

1 Which statement **best** compares the points of view of both passages?

   A. Both stories are told in first person.

   B. Both stories are told in third person.

   C. One story is told in third person, and one story is told in first person.

   D. Neither story has a point of view.

2 How does the Mariner punish the Whale? Use details from the text to support your answer.

_____

_____

_____

3 Which of the following is a true statement about how the Rhinoceros and the Whale are alike? Choose **all** that apply.

   A. Both animals are greedy.

   B. Both animals are starving and desperate.

   C. Both animals are guilty of stealing.

   D. Both animals learn a lesson.

   E. Both animals eat something they shouldn't have eaten.

   F. Both animals get advice from a fish.

4 The following question has two parts. First, answer Part A. Then, answer Part B.

Part A

Which **best** states the theme of both "How the Rhinoceros Got His Skin" and "How the Whale Got His Throat"?

A. Greed has consequences.

B. Kindness is always best.

C. Friendship is the greatest of riches.

D. Without a home, a person is lost.

Part B

Which details from the passages support the answer to Part A?

A. The shipwrecked Mariner wants the Whale to take him home, while the Parsee wants to enjoy his cake in peace.

B. The Rhinoceros is punished for eating cake that isn't his, and the Whale is punished for eating a man after he ate almost all of the fish.

C. The 'Stute Fish gives the Whale advice when the man upsets the Whale's stomach, and the Parsee warns the Rhinoceros about the dangers of eating his cake.

D. The Rhinoceros feels at home in the Red Sea, while the Mariner feels at home in the white cliffs of Albion.

5 Read the following excerpts from "How the Rhinoceros Got His Skin" and "How the Whale Got His Throat."

"How the Rhinoceros Got His Skin"
He took that skin, and he shook that skin, and he scrubbed that skin, and he rubbed that skin just as full of old, dry, stale, tickly cake-crumbs and some burned currants as ever it could possibly hold.

"How the Whale Got His Throat"
So he said to the 'Stute Fish, "This man is very nubbly, and besides he is making me hiccough. What shall I do?"

Compare and contrast the author's style in the two passages. Include at least one example of how the style is alike in the two passages, and one example of how it is different.

_____

_____

6 Both "How the Rhinoceros Got His Skin" and "How the Whale Got His Throat" are from a collection of short stories. Each has a similar topic and theme, approached in different ways. Write a paragraph that compares and contrasts the topics and themes of the passages. Include text evidence about the plots, characters, and settings to support your ideas.

Write your answer on the lines below.

_____

_____

_____

_____

_____

_____

_____

_____

_____

_____

_____

_____

Read the passage.

How Devils Tower Came to Be

In western Wyoming, there's a place called Devils Tower. If you watch carefully as you cross the prairie, you may see this massive monument sticking up on the horizon. It's a tall cone of rock that towers more than 1,200 feet over the surrounding land. This is the land of the Lakota, a tribe of Native Americans that once roamed these prairies following the buffalo herds. The Lakota know this land well, and they tell a story about the origin of Devils Tower. Only they don't call it that. Mostly, it's known as Bear Rock, which is a really good name, if you know the story. . . .

A group of Lakota was once crossing the prairie. They were in no hurry and traveled leisurely. Children chased one another and paused to play games. Two boys were playing with a ball, striking it with a stick and then racing to strike it again. Caught up in their game, they didn't keep an eye on where they were going or how far they had gotten from the group. But then they began to get hungry. They looked around, but their families were nowhere to be seen. They began walking and running, looking everywhere, but they were hopelessly lost.

The boys set off in the direction they felt was surely the right way and walked and walked and walked. For three days they walked, and still they did not see their people or any places they knew. Now and then they paused to nibble a few berries or dig up roots for food and then began walking again. What else could they do?

On the third day, as they walked along, they suddenly had the feeling that they were being followed. They both turned at once and looked around, and there following them was a monstrous bear. It was far bigger than any bear that lives today. The Lakota call him Mato, and he towered over the land like the tallest tree in the forest.

The boys began running as fast as they could, but Mato ran much faster. Soon he was almost on top of them. They could feel the bear's hot breath on their necks like a scorching summer wind blowing across the prairie. His footfalls were an earthquake that shook the earth. His roar was a thunderclap that made their ears ache.

The boys gasped for air as they ran. Their hearts beat wildly. Knowing they could never escape on their own, they called out to their creator, the Great Spirit, and the Great Spirit heard their cries. The ground shook and moved beneath their feet. A rock rose under the boys and began lifting them up into the sky.

Mato paused when he saw the rock jutting upward, but only for a moment. He would not give up his meal so easily, and he rushed toward the rock and began climbing its steep sides. In a moment, he nearly reached the top, but the rock kept rising higher and higher.

Mato, hungry and angry, kept trying to climb the rock and reach the boys. He circled the rock, trying it from every side. He left deep gashes in the sides of the rock, but he could not reach the top. Finally, Mato sat back and looked up. He was tired and hungry, and he turned and wandered off.

The boys looked down on Mato and saw him leave. Jubilant, they danced and laughed and yelled in their excitement. It was only after several minutes had passed that they began to realize that they had been saved from one awful danger but had been thrust into another. The tall, steep walls of the rock had saved them from Mato, but now it was a prison that mocked any thought they had of leaving. There was no food, no water, and no way down. They stared far out across the prairie to the distant horizon. As certainly as there had been nothing they could do to escape Mato without help, there was no way off this rock tower without help.

Once again, the boys called out to the Great Spirit, and once more he heard their cries. He called upon Wanblee, the eagle, who soared the highest of all birds in the sky. Wanblee flew to the tower and settled next to the boys. The boys climbed upon his back, and Wanblee swooped off the tower and carried the boys back to their people.

Ever since, the Lakota have told this story. And when you look up at Devils Tower today, you can almost see Mato trying to climb its steep sides. His claw marks are still there. And you may very likely see Wanblee, the eagle, circling high in the sky above Bear Rock.

Answer the following questions.

1 This question has two parts. First, answer Part A. Then, answer Part B.

Part A

Circle the **best** description of "How Devils Tower Came to Be."

Types of Fiction	contemporary fiction
	historical fiction
	science fiction
	myth

Part B

Write **one** detail from the story that supports your answer to Part A.

_____

_____

2 This question has two parts. First, answer Part A. Then, answer Part B.

Part A

Reread this paragraph from the passage.

> **On the third day, as they walked along, they suddenly had the feeling that they were being followed. They both turned at once and looked around, and there following them was a monstrous bear. It was far bigger than any bear that lives today. The Lakota call him Mato, and he towered over the land like the tallest tree in the forest.**

Based on the paragraph, what can you infer about the narrator of the story?

A. The narrator is one of the boys.

B. The narrator is not a part of the story.

C. The narrator is a member of the Lakota.

D. The narrator is the bear.

Part B

Underline **two** details in the paragraph that support your answer to Part A.

3 Underline the figurative language in each sentence. Then match the sentence to the type of figurative language on the right.

A. They could feel the bear's hot breath on their necks like a scorching summer wind blowing across the prairie.	**1.** allusion
	2. proverb
B. Caught up in their game, they didn't keep an eye on where they were going or how far they had gotten from the group.	**3.** simile
	4. adage
C. The tall, steep walls of the rock had saved them from Mato, but now it was a prison that mocked any thought they had of leaving.	**5.** metaphor
	6. idiom

4 This question has two parts. First, answer Part A. Then, answer Part B.

Part A

Which **best** states the theme of the story?

A. Young boys are likely to cause trouble.

B. A bear should be feared above all other animals.

C. The solution to a problem can become a problem itself.

D. There are often simple explanations for how places come to be.

Part B

Which detail from the story **best** supports this theme?

A. They both turned at once and looked around, and there following them was a monstrous bear.

B. The tall steep walls of the rock had saved them from Mato, but now it was a prison that mocked any thought they had of leaving.

C. He would not give up his meal so easily, and he rushed toward the rock and began climbing its steep sides.

D. A rock rose under the boys and began lifting them up into the sky.

E. Mato paused when he saw the rock jutting upward, but only for a moment.

5 This question has two parts. First, answer Part A. Then, answer Part B.

Part A

Which sentence from the story **best** describes the first conflict the boys face?

- **A.** They both turned at once and looked around, and there following them was a monstrous bear.

- **B.** There was no food, no water, and no way down.

- **C.** They began walking and running, looking everywhere, but they were hopelessly lost.

- **D.** Caught up in their game, they didn't keep an eye on where they were going or how far they had gotten from the group.

Part B

Explain how the conflict described in Part A is resolved in the story. Write your answer on the lines below.

_____

_____

_____

_____

Read the passage.

Deep in the Amazon

Mia's nose was stuck to the windowpane while her eyes searched the sky beyond. She had been sitting by the window all afternoon, staring at the sky, waiting. Her father had said he was coming for a visit and was going to take her away in his plane for an adventure.

Mia's dad hadn't lived at home for a long time, and Mia never quite knew when she might see him next. He had his own plane and traveled all the time, ferrying passengers all over the world. They often talked on the phone and exchanged text messages, but it wasn't the same as seeing him laugh and hearing his voice as he told her where he'd been and all he'd been doing. So when she got a message from him a few days earlier telling her to pack a bag, she was ecstatic.

Mia waited all afternoon and all evening, barely moving from her post at the window. Only when night fell did she finally give up on seeing Father that day. At first light the next morning, though, an airplane flew low over the house, circled, and landed in a nearby field. Father jumped out of the bright-yellow plane. "Sorry I'm late, kid," he called. "I got held up by a storm over the Atlantic, but I'm here now! Are you ready?"

Mia didn't need to be asked. Five minutes later, they were airborne.

The plane flew much faster than an ordinary plane. "It's my own design," Father explained. "It's so simple. I don't know why everyone isn't building one."

The engine roared and the ground below them streamed past in a blur as they flew over mountains, desert, and then jungle. "We're almost there," said Father. Then the engine sputtered, smoked, and died.

"Didn't expect that," Father said calmly. "It must be that rebuilt supercharger I put in last week. I thought it would last longer than this."

He tossed Mia a parachute. "Time to jump," he said and flung open the door. The clouds brushed Mia's cheeks like a silk scarf as she descended toward the forest below.

"Where are we?" Mia asked as she landed in a dense jungle.

"The Amazon rainforest," Father responded. "We should be about eighty kilometers from Manaus, an area I know. There's a scientific research team camped not far from here. We can get help from them."

Mia wondered how long it would take to walk "not far" through this wilderness they'd fallen into. Snakes and crocodile-like caimans were everywhere. Monkeys screamed from treetops as Mia struggled through the thick bushes, tangled vines, murky water, and living mud of a swamp. Mosquitoes swarmed about her like a blizzard on a winter day back home. They <u>trudged</u> on, Father tirelessly, Mia tiring quickly.

Sooner than Mia expected, they were peering at a camp nestled in a clearing. Father explained their predicament to the researchers, briefly relating his theory about the rebuilt supercharger, facts that made no sense to anyone but Father.

"We can offer you food and a place to stay," the leader said, "but we're stranded here ourselves. Our plane is grounded with mechanical problems, and our truck went into town three days ago and is still not back. We're beginning to worry."

"No problem," Father said. "If I can just look at the plane, I'll bet I can get it flying in no time. I'll fly it out of here, take Mia home, and then we'll look for that missing truck."

Mia went with her father to check out the plane. He opened the engine compartment and, in a blur of activity, retooled the engine. Then he said to the scientist, "I'll be back before you know it." He glanced at Mia. "C'mon, kid. You'll be surprised at what this plane will do now that I've worked it over."

Mia and Father jumped into the plane. The engine kicked over, and Father turned the plane and raced toward the end of the clearing, lifting the nose at the last moment and just clipping the trees as they flew over. Whatever he'd done, the plane was a roaring meteor that rocketed them into the sky and raced toward home.

As Mia watched the ground speed by, she fell into a deep sleep, and the next thing she knew, she awakened in her own bed, morning sunlight shining through her window. She remembered all that had happened. "What an extraordinary adventure!" she whispered.

She looked about her old room, where nothing had changed. Her clothes from the day before were neatly draped over a chair. "Did it really happen?" she wondered. "Did I see Father?" Just then, she heard the roar of a plane as it approached in a mad rush and circled low over the house.

Answer the following questions.

6 This question has two parts. First, answer Part A. Then, answer Part B.

Part A

Which of these statements **best** describes Mia's father?

A. He is courageous and a risk-taker.

B. He is inventive and self-assured.

C. He is honest but can be inconsiderate.

D. He is careless and unpredictable.

Part B

Write two details from the story that support your answer to Part A.

_____

_____

_____

_____

7 Read this excerpt from "Deep in the Amazon."

> Mia wondered how long it would take to walk "not far" through this wilderness they'd fallen into. Snakes and crocodile-like caimans were everywhere. Monkeys screamed from treetops as Mia struggled through the thick bushes, tangled vines, murky water, and living mud of a swamp. Mosquitoes swarmed about her like a blizzard on a winter day back home. They <u>trudged</u> on, Father tirelessly, Mia tiring quickly.

Which words and phrases in the excerpt are clues to the meaning of the word <u>trudged</u>? Choose **all** that apply.

A. struggled through

B. swarmed

C. swamp

D. back home

E. tiring quickly

8 This question has two parts. First, answer Part A. Then, answer Part B.

Part A

Which of the following **best** describes something you might infer by reading the last paragraph of the story?

A. Mia's adventure was all a dream.

B. Mia's father doesn't really know how to fly a plane.

C. Mia's father isn't coming to visit after all.

D. Mia didn't get any sleep the previous evening.

Part B

Underline **one** detail in the paragraph that helped you make the inference you chose in Part A.

9 How does the setting in both "How Devils Tower Came to Be" and "Deep in the Amazon" provide a common challenge for the characters? Cite textual evidence from both passages.

Write your answer on the lines provided.

_____

_____

_____

_____

_____

_____

PERFORMANCE TASK

"How Devils Tower Came to Be" tells an origin story from long ago. "Deep in the Amazon" is set in a more modern time period. As different as the settings of these stories are, they share a similar characteristic: The characters seem real even as they are placed in fantastical situations. Write an essay comparing and contrasting how the characters in each story react to and resolve the conflicts they face during their adventures. In what ways are their actions believable?

Remember to use textual evidence to support your ideas. Write your answer on the lines below.

STRAND
2

Working with Informational Texts

RI.5.2, RI.5.5, L.5.4.b

Articles

Nonfiction is writing about real people, places, events, or things. Because it gives readers information or facts, it is sometimes called **informational text**. There are many types of nonfiction.

Type of Nonfiction	Purpose
biography	to tell the true story of a person's life
essay	to share the author's outlook or point of view
speech	to present a topic that is shared orally
textbook	to give factual information about a topic

One common type of nonfiction is an **article**. You can find articles in newspapers, magazines, and online. Every nonfiction article has a **main idea** that tells what the text is mostly about. **Evidence** is information that supports the main idea. Types of evidence include examples, facts, and quotes. Each paragraph also has a main idea and details that support the main idea of a passage. When you **summarize** a passage, you retell the main ideas in your own words. Read the following passage. Circle the main idea of each paragraph and underline the evidence used to support the main idea.

> Riding a bicycle can be dangerous. More children ages five to fourteen are injured in cycling accidents than in any other sport. In fact, nearly three hundred thousand children are injured each year.
>
> Be safe when you ride. Ride on the right side of the road with the flow of traffic. Obey all traffic signs and signals. Most importantly, wear a bike helmet.

When you read informational texts, you can use the available facts and details to make an inference. An **inference** is a decision based on text evidence and personal knowledge.

Text Structure

When authors write articles, they keep their readers in mind. Their purpose is to inform readers about a topic, so they use formal language and present facts in an objective way. This means the author stays neutral and doesn't express opinions.

To make information easier to understand, authors carefully organize how they present that information. How an author organizes a text is called **structure**. The structure helps you connect ideas in a text and better understand how parts of the text relate to the whole passage. Different structures present information in different ways.

Chronological Order The author presents events in the order in which events happened, or in **sequence**. Authors often use **chronological order**, or time sequence, to organize their writing. Dates and time-order words, such as *first*, *next*, and *last*, signal when things happen. Read the following passage and circle the words that provide clues about sequence.

> Pluto was once the ninth planet in our solar system. Then, in 2006, scientists defined a planet as an object with a clear orbit around a star. Since Pluto does not have a clear orbit, it was reclassified. Today it is classified as a dwarf planet.

Cause and Effect The author shows the **cause**, or reason something happens, and its **effect**, or what happens as a result. Signal words, such as *because*, and *therefore*, can help you understand a cause and its effect. Read the following passage. Underline the cause and circle the effect.

> Temperatures are very high beneath Earth's crust. Because temperatures are so high, they melt rock. This melted rock is called *magma*.

Problem and Solution The author states a **problem** and then presents a **solution**, or how the problem can be solved. Read the following passage. Underline the problem and circle the solution.

> Many pioneers who settled the Great Plains lived in sod houses built from thick-rooted prairie grasses. This was because the prairie lacked standard building materials, such as wood or stone.

Compare and Contrast When authors **compare**, they tell how things are alike. When authors **contrast**, they tell how things are different. This structure uses signal words such as *similarly* and *in contrast* to show the relationship between ideas. Read the following passage. Underline the objects being compared.

> Most reptiles lay eggs. The shell of a reptile egg is not hard like the shell of a bird's egg. Instead, a reptile's egg is soft and leathery.

Text and Graphic Features

A **text feature**, such as bold print and a heading, helps readers locate information quickly. A **graphic feature** is something that helps readers visualize information. Text and graphic features may include:

- a heading, which tells readers what a section of text is about and how it relates to the passage.
- a photograph, which helps readers visualize a topic.
- a caption, which explains what a photograph shows.
- a diagram, which is a drawing that shows the different parts of something, such as a machine or the human heart.
- a graph or chart, which shows facts or information in a visual way.
- a map, which is a picture that shows the location of things or places.

Language Spotlight • Affixes and Roots

A **root** is a meaningful word or word part that can be used to make a longer word. Many roots come from Latin or Greek. Roots that can stand on their own are called base words. An **affix** is a letter or group of letters added to a root to create a new meaning. An affix added to the beginning of a word is a **prefix**. An affix added to the end of a word is a **suffix**.

Use what you know about affixes and roots to define the underlined words below. Then use a dictionary to verify the meaning of the words.

Some marine biologists use small submarines to explore the habitats of sea creatures.

Read the passage.

Ben Oppenheimer: Planet Hunter

Have you ever looked up at the night sky? Do you wonder what is out there? We know our sun is not the only star in the sky. We also know there are planets outside of our solar system. But what are these planets like? Could they support life?

Ben Oppenheimer wondered about these same questions. He was so curious that he became an astrophysicist. An astrophysicist is a scientist who studies the nature of stars and planets. The word comes from Greek: *astro* means "stars" and *phys* means "nature."

Faraway Worlds

Oppenheimer studies planets at the American Museum of Natural History in New York City. His special interest is extrasolar planets, commonly referred to as exoplanets. These are planets that circle stars other than our sun. He and other scientists have already found more than eight hundred extrasolar planets. There may be thousands more.

The nearest extrasolar planet is about 25 trillion miles from Earth, too far away for people to visit. As a result, scientists have come up with a different way to study these exoplanets.

Seeing in Space

Oppenheimer and other scientists learn about extrasolar planets by studying the light they give off. Special telescopes and cameras can capture this light and make images of it. But the field of extrasolar planet study is new and the instruments are crude, so Oppenheimer spends a lot of time developing better tools.

One difficulty Oppenheimer had was being able to clearly see the faint light from an extrasolar planet. "The main problem is that the stars are hundreds of millions to billions of times brighter than the planets that orbit them," Oppenheimer said in a recent article. "So the glare of the star wipes out any hope of really seeing the planets."

To solve this problem, Oppenheimer invented a camera that blocks starlight, allowing the light from the planets to come through. "Think about having a bright light shining in your face," Oppenheimer explains. "If you hold your hand up to block the light, you can see better."

Now, Oppenheimer hopes that he and his team can use this camera to find many new planets—maybe even a planet like Earth that could support life.

Like our sun, some stars have planets that orbit them. This illustration shows an exoplanet and its sun.

Answer the following questions.

1 Read all parts of the question before responding.

Part A

Which main idea is developed in the passage? Choose **all** that apply.

A. Oppenheimer looks for planets that orbit stars other than our sun.

B. Oppenheimer studies planets at the American Museum of Natural History.

C. Oppenheimer invents many of the tools he uses to help him study exoplanets.

D. Oppenheimer studies the light that exoplanets give off to learn about them.

Part B

Underline details in the passage that support the answer to Part A.

Part C

Use the answers to Part A and Part B to write a summary of the passage.

Write your answer on the lines provided.

_____

_____

> **Hint** A main idea is what the author wants readers to learn about a topic.

2 Read the problem in each choice. Then, match each problem to its solution on the right.

A. Ben Oppenheimer wanted to learn about planets outside our solar system.	**1.** Oppenheimer spends a lot of time developing better instruments.
B. Glare from stars blocked out the light from exoplanets.	**2.** Oppenheimer invented a camera that blocks starlight but not the light from exoplanets.
C. Instruments for exoplanet study are crude.	**3.** Oppenheimer became an astrophysicist.

> **Hint** Look for words such as *problem* and *solve* to help you identify problems and solutions.

3 The following question has two parts. First, answer Part A. Then, answer Part B.

Part A

Which **best** explains what *exo* in exoplanet means?

A. inside

C. opposite

B. extra

D. outside

Part B

Which **best** defines exoplanet, as it is used in the passage?

A. a planet inside our solar system

B. a planet outside our solar system

C. a planet that is not like other planets

D. a planet that has extra features

Hint The passage says an exoplanet is a planet that circles a star other than our own. Use this information to help define the prefix.

4 The following question has two parts. First, answer Part A. Then, answer Part B.

Part A

Which text and graphic features are used in the passage? Choose **all** that apply.

A. heading

D. illustration

B. caption

E. diagram

C. graph

F. map

Part B

Explain how the text and graphic features in the answer to Part A help you better understand the text.

_____

_____

Hint Remember that text features help readers locate information quickly, and graphic features present information visually.

Use the Reading Guide to help you understand the passage.

Music from Garbage

Reading Guide

What do you learn about the children of Cateura In the section "Why Trash?"

In what ways is trash an important part of life in Cateura?

Why is the outlook for children living in Cateura grim?

Juan Manuel Chavez picks up his cello. His bow touches the strings, and strains of Bach fill the air. If you closed your eyes, you might think you are listening to a cellist on stage in a grand symphony hall. But Juan Manuel is nineteen years old, and his cello is constructed from an oil can and wood that were thrown out in the garbage.

Why Trash?

Juan Manuel is part of "The Recycled Orchestra," a youth orchestra in the South American country of Paraguay. Juan Manuel's cello isn't the only instrument in the orchestra made of trash. A violin is made from a bowl and a block of wood with strings held in place by a fork. A flute is made from a metal pipe and a spoon. In fact, all the instruments are made from trash.

The twenty-five young musicians in "The Recycled Orchestra" live in Cateura, one of the poorest towns in South America. Located right outside the Paraguayan capital, Asuncion, Cateura is the city's landfill. Its 2,500 families live in the midst of the garbage next to a polluted river full of toxic chemicals.

Each day 1,500 tons of garbage are dumped at Cateura. To earn a living, many residents separate the trash and sell it. They also use the garbage to build their homes. Not surprisingly, the outlook for children who live there is grim. Nearly half of them must leave school because their families need them to work.

The musicians in "The Recycled Orchestra" live near a landfill like this one.

Reading Guide

What signal words in the section "From Humble Beginnings" provide clues about its text structure?

Think about the quotes the author includes. What do these quotes suggest about the author's feelings toward the topic?

From Humble Beginnings

Aiming to keep Cateura's children safe and out of trouble, music teacher Favio Chavez opened a music school there in 2007. But with only five instruments to share, the students often got bored.

Real instruments were too expensive. "A community like Cateura is not a place to have a violin," Chavez said. "In fact, a violin is worth more than a house here." Chavez asked one of the town's residents to make instruments from trash.

With recycled instruments in hand, Chavez and his students got busy. "At first it was very difficult because we had no place to rehearse, and we had to teach in the same place where the parents were working in the trash," said Chavez.

Since then, more than 120 children have learned to play musical instruments. Currently Chavez has about fifty students, about half of whom make up the orchestra.

Today "The Recycled Orchestra" is internationally acclaimed. Their performances in various countries have drawn attention and praise. A film has been made about them. And the Musical Instruments Museum in Arizona is setting up a permanent exhibit of their recycled instruments.

A Brighter Future

Chavez sees the orchestra as a way to a better life for its members and their families. "We are at a time when they definitely are changing their lives through the orchestra," Chavez said. "We dream that families and children can have a better house and Internet access, so they can connect with opportunities."

The orchestra helps its members find confidence and hope. "Music causes children to connect and feel they are building something together," Chavez said. "Our orchestra feels special because the children make beauty out of garbage."

The young people seem to agree. "When I listen to the sound of a violin, I feel butterflies in my stomach," said Ada Maribel Rios Bordados, a thirteen-year-old violin player. "It's a feeling I don't know how to explain."

A fellow musician added, "My life would be worthless without music."

Answer the following questions.

1 Read this sentence from the passage.

Not surprisingly, the outlook for children who live [in Cateura] is grim.

Which excerpt from the passage supports this statement? Choose **all** that apply.

A. Juan Manuel is part of "The Recycled Orchestra," a youth orchestra . . .

B. A flute is made from a metal pipe and a spoon.

C. The twenty-five young musicians in "The Recycled Orchestra" live in Cateura . . .

D. Its 2,500 families live in the midst of the garbage next to a polluted river . . .

E. Nearly half of them must leave school because their families need them to work.

2 Which main idea is developed in the passage? Choose **all** that apply.

A. Aiming to keep Cateura's children safe and out of trouble, music teacher Favio Chavez opened a music school there in 2007.

B. With recycled instruments in hand, Chavez and his students got busy.

C. "We are at a time when they definitely are changing their lives through the orchestra," Chavez said.

D. Chavez sees the orchestra as a way to a better life for its members and their families.

3 What inference can you make about how the author views the topic of the passage? Use details from the passage to support your response.

Write your answer on the lines provided.

_____

_____

_____

4 The following question has two parts. First, answer Part A. Then, answer Part B.

Part A

What does the word <u>internationally</u> mean, as it is used in the passage?

A. including all nations

B. relating to one nation

C. involving more than one nation

D. inside one nation

Part B

Which affixes help the reader understand the meaning of <u>internationally</u>?

A. the prefix *inter-* meaning "between or among" and the suffix *-ly* meaning "in a way that is"

B the prefix *in-* meaning "not" and the suffix *-al* meaning "relating to"

C. the prefix *intro-* meaning "inside" and the suffix *-al* meaning "relating to"

D. the prefix *terr-* meaning "earth or land" and the suffix *-ly* meaning "in a way that is"

5 Read the following sentence from the passage.

A fellow musician added, "My life would be worthless without music."

What inference can you make about this musician's life? Why might he or she have made this statement? Use details from the passage to support your response.

Write your answer on the lines below.

_____

_____

_____

_____

6 What is the overall text structure of "Ben Oppenheimer: Planet Hunter" and of "Music from Garbage"? Compare and contrast how the authors of both passages use text structure to organize and present information. Use details from the passages to support your response.

Write your answer on the lines below.

_____

_____

_____

_____

_____

_____

_____

_____

_____

_____

_____

_____

_____

_____

_____

_____

_____

RI.5.6, RI.5.8, RI.5.9, L.5.5.a

Persuasive Texts

1 GETTING THE IDEA

Persuasive text is written to persuade, or convince, readers to accept a certain view or take a specific action. Persuasive texts include speeches, arguments, essays, and opinion blog posts. One place that often features persuasive texts is the editorial section of a newspaper or magazine. Editors give their opinions in **editorials**. Readers respond to news stories by writing **letters to the editor**.

Structure

Many persuasive texts follow this common structure:

- An **introduction**, which states the author's position.

- **Supporting paragraphs** with reasons and evidence to back up the author's position.

- A **conclusion**, which restates the author's position and summarizes the main points.

In a persuasive text, an author gives his or her **point of view,** or personal beliefs about a topic. At the beginning of the text, the author makes a claim. A **claim** is a statement an author makes in support of or against an idea. The remainder of the text will explain more about the author's claim.

Reasons and Evidence

An author of a persuasive text wants readers to accept his or her ideas. He or she will lay out specific reasons that explain to readers why they should consider his or her point of view. Each **reason** is a statement that tells why the claim is worthy or important. Well-written persuasive texts usually have multiple reasons to support each claim.

In addition, each reason should be supported by evidence. **Evidence** includes facts, examples, details, data, or other information that show why the author believes the claim. A good author will present strong, convincing evidence. This demonstrates that the author has carefully considered all information to form a complete idea about the topic. When the evidence is solid, readers are more likely to believe what the author has to say.

The following chart shows an author's claim and the reasons and evidence used to support it.

Claim: Our state should not charge tolls on state highways.		
Reason: Paying tolls slows down traffic and creates traffic back-ups.	**Reason:** Having tollbooths increases the number of accidents on the highway.	**Reason:** Citizens cannot afford to pay the high tolls that are part of their daily commutes.
Evidence: Drivers frequently report slowed or stopped traffic in the miles before a tollbooth.	**Evidence:** More accidents occur within the miles before and after a tollbooth than on any other part of the highway.	**Evidence:** The average citizen with an hour commute can spend as much as $1,000 a year on highway tolls.

Though authors of informational texts rely on **facts**, or statements that can be proved, persuasive authors often include opinions in their work. **Opinions** are statements of personal belief. They cannot be proved. Authors may include opinions that are supported by facts and details, but that does not make them true. As you read a persuasive text, be careful to separate information that is true from statements of personal thoughts and feelings.

When you consider an author's claim, you should also make sure that all the evidence is **relevant**, or closely related to the topic. For example, a student writes that too much homework has negative effects on students. In the essay, the student states that more hours of homework are associated with fewer hours of sleep. Which of the following evidence would NOT be relevant to the author's claim?

- statistics from research studies about students' sleep habits

- accounts from students about how too much homework has affected their sleep

- a quote from a student about how homework is unfair

Persuasive Techniques

Writers of persuasive texts present their claims and evidence in different ways than in other texts. They use language that is designed to influence the reader. These methods, called **persuasive techniques**, often appeal to the reader's emotions or sense of right and wrong. The chart below shows other examples of persuasive techniques.

Technique	What It Does	Example
bandwagon appeal	implies that "everyone is doing it, so you should, too"	Most Americans prefer to drink bottled water over tap water.
generalizations	makes a broad statement that may not apply to all people or things described	We all know that people should drink eight glasses of water every day.
famous names	uses a celebrity's or expert's name to promote something	Dr. Sam, host of the TV show *Get Healthy*, drinks this brand of water.

Always consider whether an author may be biased. When an author is **biased**, he or she slants the information to benefit a personal interest. Ask: *What might the author gain from persuading people to change their views? Does this affect how he or she presents the information?*

Language Spotlight • Figurative Language

Many persuasive writers use **figurative language** to draw a comparison that readers can relate to or that can affect readers' emotions. Circle each example of figurative language below.

Is your rock of a mattress causing you aches and pains? Then you need to try our cushion foam mattresses! Sleeping on one of our mattresses is like snuggling into a puffy cloud.

Read the passage.

Digital Textbooks Are the Way of the Future

Schools across the country should switch from regular textbooks to digital textbooks. Regular textbooks are too heavy for students to carry around and don't offer timely information. They are also very expensive in the long run. New e-readers are much more convenient and more likely to be read by today's youth.

First of all, loading textbooks onto an e-reader is much more convenient than lugging around a stack of heavy textbooks. Studies also show that heavy backpacks can be bad for students' bodies. Specifically, one recent study at the University of California used MRI[1] scans to show that overloaded backpacks place stress on the spine. This can cause the spine to curve and lead to lasting damage. Why slump under the weight of a heavy bag when you can carry all of your books in one small device? An e-reader is much more sensible and convenient. Not only is it small and lightweight, but it can carry all of a students' books along with a lot of other content.

In addition to being heavy, textbooks are also expensive. Because of books' high prices, schools often limit how often books are replaced. As a result, books can quickly become outdated or show damage from overuse. On the other hand, e-readers can be easily and quickly updated using the Internet. This means that students and schools can readily access the most up-to-date educational resources. And many of these resources are offered at a reduced cost. Plenty of experts agree that schools can save a lot of money by using e-readers. Sure, the start-up fees to purchase the e-readers may be steep, but the long-term savings are well worth the initial costs.

[1] **MRI**: "Magnetic Resonance Imaging"; a medical imaging system that uses a magnetic field and energy waves to take pictures of the inside of the human body.

Most likely, schools would not have to purchase e-readers for all students. Many parents and students already own e-readers or tablets that can store e-books. Reading on a digital device has become a common practice for most people. Many newspapers and magazines now rely on digital subscribers to keep their publications going. In all likelihood, e-books will one day replace paper books in the same way that digital music has largely replaced CDs. Schools should stay ahead of this trend and make the switch now.

By using e-readers, schools can better appeal to students' interests and motivate them to read. A majority of students are immersed in the current digital trends. So it is likely that they would be more motivated to read their assignments if they could do so on a digital device.

Overall, it only makes sense for schools to replace their textbooks with e-readers. Not only can e-readers save schools time and money, but they can save students from strained backs, too! On top of that, they are fun and motivating for students. That reason alone should justify the switch. After all, we all want to do what's best for students' learning!

Answer the following questions.

1 Which sentence from the passage includes the **best** example of a persuasive technique?

A. This can cause the spine to curve and lead to lasting damage.

B. Why slump under the weight of a heavy bag when you can carry all of your books in one small device?

C. In addition to being heavy, textbooks are also expensive.

D. Many newspapers and magazines now rely on digital subscribers to keep their publications going.

Hint Think about which sentence asks the reader to feel something in response to the topic.

2 This question has two parts. First, answer Part A. Then, answer Part B.

Part A

What is the author's claim?

A. Students should read more books.

B. Schools do not buy enough textbooks.

C. Schools should replace print textbooks with digital textbooks.

D. E-readers are more convenient than textbooks.

Part B

Which excerpt from the passage **best** supports the answer to Part A?

A. Schools across the country should switch from regular textbooks to digital textbooks.

B. First of all, loading textbooks onto an e-reader is much more convenient than lugging around a stack of heavy textbooks.

C. Because of books' high prices, schools often limit how often they are replaced.

D. Many parents and students already own e-readers or tablets that can store e-books.

Hint Look at the claim you chose in Part A. Choose the excerpt from the passage that states the author's claim.

3 Read the sentences below. Then match each sentence to the idea it supports on the right.

A. Specifically, one recent study at the University of California used MRI scans to show that overloaded backpacks place stress on the spine.

1. E-books are more up-to-date than textbooks.

B. On the other hand, e-readers can be easily and quickly updated using the Internet.

2. E-readers are more cost effective than regular books.

C. Plenty of experts agree that schools can save a lot of money by using e-readers.

3. Textbooks are too heavy for students to carry.

> **Hint** Think about each reason on the right. How does the author support the idea with facts, examples, or other data?

4 Describe how the author structured the passage. Use details from the passage to support your response.

Write your answer on the lines provided.

_____

_____

_____

_____

_____

_____

_____

_____

Use the Reading Guide to help you understand the passage.

Print Textbooks Belong in the Classroom

Duplicating any part of this book is prohibited by law. © 2015 Triumph Learning, LLC

Reading Guide

Notice how the author introduces the topic. How might this introduction affect the reader's view of the topic?

What is the author's claim?

What evidence does the author provide as evidence to support his or her claim?

Picture a classroom in which each student holds a digital device in his or her hand. The class is doing a group reading of *Johnny Tremain*. But what is actually happening on each device? One student is playing a game, and another is typing a private note. Several students are having technical problems and can't get their devices to turn to the right page. Sounds like a nightmare for any student or teacher. Yet, this will be the reality if schools switch to digital books. Print textbooks are more appropriate for classroom learning and should not be replaced by electronic textbooks.

As the example above shows, digital books would be a distraction in schools. The majority of digital devices contain games and other applications that would distract students from reading. Even e-readers, devices designed for reading books, usually include other features. Research shows that young adult brains are less able to focus on one task than adult brains. So why would schools want to increase the distractions students face?

In addition to being distracting, e-readers may impede learning simply because they use screens. One study by the University of Leicester showed this. Some students read about an unfamiliar subject on e-readers and other students read the same material in print. The results of the study showed that students who read the printed books learned the information more quickly. Other researchers have also looked into these differences. They have found that the brain processes digital text differently than printed text. In the long run, digital devices may negatively affect students' learning.

Why does the author give an example of a school district with two thousand students?

What does the author say about requiring students to use their own equipment?

How does the author show a possible bias?

Why might someone disagree with the author's reasons?

Beyond these possible effects on learning, reading on screens can also hurt people's eyes. In a recent study by Indiana State University, many students who read on digital devices complained of eye strain. This is a common problem for many users of technology. Doctors blame "computer vision syndrome" on several factors, including smaller print sizes and bright screens. Supporters of e-readers claim that e-readers help eliminate the back strain of heavy backpacks. But, clearly it is a trade-off. An e-reader may not cause back pain, but it can hurt the eyes instead.

Yet, even if you dismiss these negative effects, there are several basic problems that make e-readers a bad idea for schools. First and foremost, e-readers are expensive. Their prices range from $79 to more than $500. So, imagine how much it would cost to purchase a device for every student. In a school district of two thousand students, the cost could be anywhere from $158,000 to one million dollars! And these high fees are just for the devices alone. Purchasing the actual e-books would cost even more. Most school budgets do not have the means for this.

Some people may suggest that students use their own digital devices for reading e-books at school. Although it may be true that many students have e-reading devices at home, there are also many students who do not. It would be unfair to require students to have their own e-reading equipment.

Reading Guide

What e-reader technical problems does the author mention? Why does the author include this?

How does the author use persuasive techniques in the conclusion?

What final thought does the author give the reader? What impact might this have on the reader?

Despite e-readers' high price, they do not always function well. Paper books may sustain damage over time, but they do not malfunction like technology does. E-readers can experience problems with software and hardware. Programs may not run correctly or the device may freeze up and stop working. Digital e-readers also run on batteries. They constantly need to be recharged. If a student or teacher forgets to recharge a device, it may die in the middle of class time. Schools' technology support teams are busy enough with all the other technology issues in schools. Any additional equipment would require more support staff, which also means an additional cost for schools.

Aside from technical problems, e-readers may also break if students do not take proper care of them. Many people think e-readers' small size and light weight are positive features. However, these traits also make e-readers fragile. The screen or internal parts are likely to break if the device is dropped or stepped on. And even if a student takes proper care of his or her e-reader, the device may get stolen or lost. Because e-readers are costly, they are associated with high rates of theft.

While e-readers may have some good features, the possible negative effects of using e-readers clearly outweigh any potential benefits for schools. Replacing print textbooks with digital ones will hurt students' attention, learning, and even their eyes! And the cost of the digital e-readers, e-books, and increased technology support will hurt schools' budgets. It only makes sense to avoid these hassles and keep print books in the classroom. Unlike e-textbooks, printed textbooks will not crash, break, or run out of batteries. They will always be there when you need them.

Answer the following questions.

1 Use the statements from the box to complete the chart showing how the author introduces and supports the claim in "Print Textbooks Belong in the Classroom."

> It would be too expensive for schools to use e-readers.
>
> Purchasing the actual e-books would be an additional cost.
>
> Print books should not be replaced with electronic textbooks.
>
> E-readers range in price from $79 to more than $500.

Claim	
Reason	
Evidence	

2 Write **two** details from the passage that have examples of persuasive techniques.

_____

_____

_____

_____

_____

3 The following question has two parts. First, answer Part A. Then, answer Part B.

Part A

Which sentence from the passage **does not** support the author's claim?

A. The majority of digital devices contain games and other applications that would distract students from reading.

B. Supporters of e-readers claim that e-readers help eliminate the back strain of heavy backpacks.

C. Even if a student takes proper care of his or her e-reader, the device may get stolen or lost.

D. The possible negative effects of using e-readers clearly outweigh any potential benefits for schools.

Part B

Which statement does the author make to argue against the claim in the answer to Part A?

A. However, these traits also make e-readers very fragile.

B. Unlike e-textbooks, printed textbooks will not crash, break, or run out of batteries.

C. An e-reader may not cause back pain, but it can hurt the eyes instead.

D. Because e-readers are costly, they are associated with high rates of theft.

4 The following question has two parts. First, answer Part A. Then, answer Part B.

Part A

Read the following excerpt from the passage.

> **But what is actually happening on each device? One student is playing a game, and another is typing a private note. Several students are having technical problems and can't get their devices to turn to the right page. Sounds like a nightmare for any student or teacher. Yet, this will be the reality if schools switch to digital books.**

Underline the figurative phrase the author uses.

Part B

How does the author expect to affect the reader's reaction by making the comparison in the answer to Part A?

_____

_____

_____

5 Which of the following **best** supports the author's view that e-readers do not always function well? Choose **all** that apply.

A. The majority of digital devices contain games and other applications that would distract students from reading.

B. Their prices range from $79 to more than $500.

C. E-readers can experience problems with software and hardware.

D. If a student or teacher forgets to recharge a device, it may die in the middle of class time.

E. Many people think e-readers' small size and light weight are positive features.

6 The authors of "Digital Textbooks Are the Way of the Future" and "Print Textbooks Belong in the Classroom" both address whether schools should use digital textbooks. Compare and contrast each author's point of view about this topic and the reasons and evidence each author uses to support his or her point of view. Use details from both passages to support your response.

Write your answer on the lines below.

_____

_____

_____

_____

_____

_____

_____

_____

_____

_____

_____

_____

_____

_____

Historical Texts

① GETTING THE IDEA

Historical text is writing about people and events from the past. When you read historical texts, you look for facts and evidence in both records from the past and writings from the present. From this **evidence**, or proof, you begin to understand what life was like at a certain time. Here are a few types of historical text.

Type of Historical Text	Purpose
diary	tells about the daily activities of the person writing it; shares personal thoughts
letter	communicates information between people
newspaper article	gives factual information about a topic
biography/autobiography	provides factual information about a person's life

Authors of historical texts may write to:

- inform readers about people, events, or ideas from the past.
- inform readers about current people, events, or ideas.
- persuade readers to take action.
- influence government officials.
- encourage social change.

An author's **point of view** is how he or she considers or observes a topic or event. People with different points of view have different opinions about the same topic or event. When authors present all facts and details fairly, they present an **objective point of view**. When authors select the facts they use based on their own personal opinions or in order to influence a reader, they are writing from a **subjective point of view**. Subjective writing contains bias. **Bias** is a belief in one way of thinking or being partial to something.

Read the following excerpt from a speech. What is the author's purpose and point of view? Underline words and phrases that support your answer.

> *excerpted and adapted from*
> ## John F. Kennedy's Inaugural Address
>
> . . . In the long history of the world, only a few generations have been granted the role of defending freedom in its hour of maximum danger. I do not shrink from this responsibility—I welcome it. I do not believe that any of us would exchange places with any other people or any other generation. The energy, the faith, the devotion which we bring to this endeavor will light our country and all who serve it—and the glow from that fire can truly light the world.
>
> And so, my fellow Americans: ask not what your country can do for you—ask what you can do for your country.

Text Structure

Authors use **text structure** to organize information in a text. These structures help readers understand how people, events, and ideas are related.

- A **chronological structure** presents ideas and concepts in time order. In historical texts, authors often use dates to relate when events happened. Biographies and autobiographies often rely on a chronological structure.

- A **compare-and-contrast structure** explores how two or more topics are alike and different. Words such as *alike*, *both*, *as well as*, *unlike*, *however*, and *instead of* are used in this kind of structure. A social studies textbook might compare and contrast individuals or a place before and after an event.

- A **cause-and-effect structure** explains an event—the cause—and what happens as a result—the effect. Words such as *because*, *since*, *as a result*, *due to*, and *if . . . then* help organize this text structure. A president's speech explaining the reasons for signing a bill into law might follow this structure.

- A **problem-and-solution structure** presents a problem and explains how it is, or could be, solved. This type of structure often uses words such as *reason*, *in order to*, and *so that*. An article explaining how an ancient city had limited water so it built aqueducts and fountains to bring water there is an example of this structure.

Graphic Features

Historical texts often use graphic features to help clarify information in a text. **Graphic features** can help you visualize what you are reading or help you understand an aspect of the topic.

- A **timeline** records specific events that happen over a period of time.

First Five States to Secede from the United States (1860–1861)

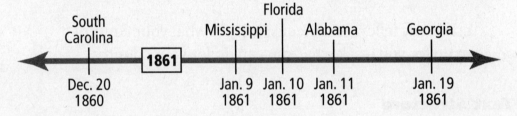

- A **graph** shows facts or information in a visual way. It uses sections, bars, or lines to compare and contrast ideas or show how ideas relate to one another.

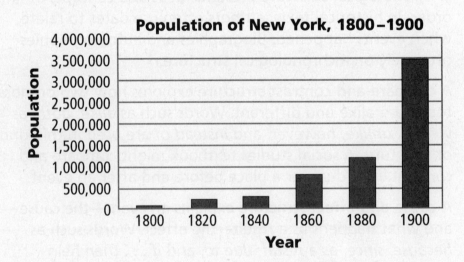

- A **map** displays the location of things or places.

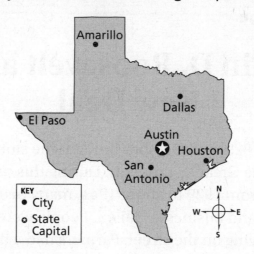

- A **flowchart** shows the sequence of steps in a process or how things relate to one another by using arrows or connecting lines.

Basic Economic Cycle Model

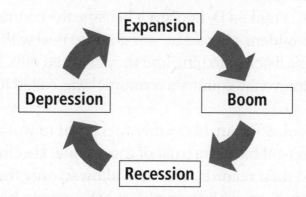

Language Spotlight • Domain-Specific Vocabulary

Like most subject-area texts, historical texts contain **domain-specific vocabulary**, or words that are specific to a topic. For example, the words *amendment* and *bill* are words you might see when reading about government. Read the following paragraph. Use context to define the underlined word. Then use a dictionary to verify its meaning.

The authors of the United States Constitution organized a government and wrote its basic laws. To help get the Constitution passed by the states, they added a Bill of Rights. The ten amendments in the Bill of Rights describe basic freedoms protected by the Constitution.

Read the passage.

Franklin D. Roosevelt and the New Deal

The year was 1929, and October brought the stock market[1] crash and the start of the Great Depression. During this depression,[2] which stretched from 1929 to about 1941, many people lost their jobs. Banks and businesses failed. People were hungry and often ended up living on the street. Farmers had a hard time, too. Beginning around 1931, the Great Plains part of the country experienced a severe drought.[3] Crops died, and dust from land that had been plowed began to blow across the farms. The Great Plains became the Dust Bowl.

Then in 1932, Franklin D. Roosevelt became the country's thirty-second president. He said he was going to deal with the nation's problems. People listened to him, and they believed him. Roosevelt's plan to help improve the country's economy[4] was called the New Deal.

Roosevelt took office in 1933 and quickly got to work. First, he helped banks get back the trust of the people. He closed the banks, checked their records, and then allowed only the strongest banks to reopen. Next, with the support of Congress, he created programs that would get people working again. Starting in 1933 and continuing throughout much of the 1930s, he and Congress established programs to improve people's lives and the economy.

[1] **stock market**: a place where people buy and sell stocks or shares in companies

[2] **depression**: a time in which the economy does not grow

[3] **drought**: a period of little or no rain

[4] **economy**: the way people in a country use resources to meet their needs

Some New Deal programs, such as the Farm Security Administration (FSA) and the Tennessee Valley Authority (TVA) helped poor farmers. The FSA bought unsuccessful farms and relocated farmers to areas that were more suitable for farming. The TVA made efforts to modernize rural areas, particularly in Tennessee, by providing electricity, controlling floods, developing economic programs, and more. Other programs were meant to help people in the 1930s and into the future. These included the Social Security Act and the Fair Labor Standards Act. The Social Security Act gave federal money to the elderly to try to prevent poverty in old age. The Fair Labor Standards Act mandated a maximum forty-four-hour work week, established a minimum wage, guaranteed overtime wages, and protected minors through child labor laws.

From 1933 until his death in 1945, President Roosevelt kept his promise to the voters and helped them with his "New Deal."

This timeline shows when some New Deal programs began.

Timeline of Some New Deal Programs

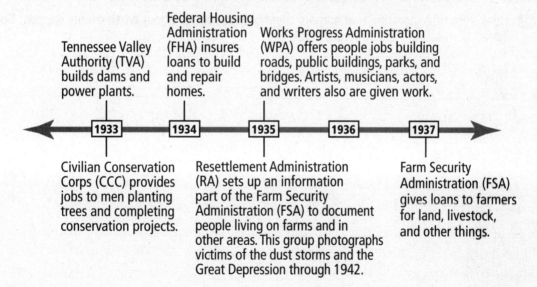

Tennessee Valley Authority (TVA) builds dams and power plants.

Federal Housing Administration (FHA) insures loans to build and repair homes.

Works Progress Administration (WPA) offers people jobs building roads, public buildings, parks, and bridges. Artists, musicians, actors, and writers also are given work.

1933 1934 1935 1936 1937

Civilian Conservation Corps (CCC) provides jobs to men planting trees and completing conservation projects.

Resettlement Administration (RA) sets up an information part of the Farm Security Administration (FSA) to document people living on farms and in other areas. This group photographs victims of the dust storms and the Great Depression through 1942.

Farm Security Administration (FSA) gives loans to farmers for land, livestock, and other things.

Answer the following questions.

1 This question has two parts. First, answer Part A. Then, answer Part B.

Part A

What is the overall text structure of the passage?

A. cause and effect

B. chronological

C. compare and contrast

D. problem and solution

Part B

Which phrase from the passage **best** supports the answer to Part A?

A. During this depression

B. Then in 1932

C. became the country's thirty-second president

D. was called the New Deal

> **Hint** Think about the structure that authors commonly use to tell about when events happen. Does the author use that text structure here?

2 Explain the author's point of view on the topic of the passage. Use at least **two** details from the passage or timeline to support your answer.

_____

_____

_____

_____

_____

Hint What does the author think about President Roosevelt's programs? How do you know?

3 Which **best** explains why the author included a timeline as part of the passage?

  A. to show when specific New Deal programs were created over a period of time

  B. to explain how the New Deal programs improved people's lives

  C. to illustrate the purpose of all the New Deal programs

  D. to compare and contrast the different New Deal programs

Hint Think about the purpose of a timeline. Why would an author include a timeline in a historical text?

4 The following events are from the passage and timeline. Write the number 2, 3, 4, or 5 so that the events are in the correct order.

| 1 | The Great Depression begins. |

| | The Federal Housing Administration (FHA) begins insuring loans for home repairs and other construction projects. |

| | The Resettlement Administration (RA) sets up an information part of the Farm Security Administration (FSA) to document people living on farms. |

| | Farmers' crops die, and dust begins to spread throughout the Great Plains. |

| | President Roosevelt closes banks, checks their records, and allows only the strongest to reopen. |

| 6 | The Farm Security Administration (FSA) gives loans to farmers for land, livestock, and other things. |

Hint Refer back to the text and timeline, looking for when each listed event occurred. Write the dates next to the events to help you order them.

Use the Reading Guide to help you understand the passage.

Photographing History

Duplicating any part of this book is prohibited by law. © 2015 Triumph Learning, LLC

Reading Guide

Look for words that indicate text structure such as *first*, *because*, or *reason*. These words can help you determine the structure of the passage.

What are the results of Lange's actions?

During what decade did most of the events happen?

Dorothea Lange was born in 1895 in New Jersey. However, her story really begins at the age of nineteen when she received her first camera. She had been working for a photographer, and he gave her a camera. That gift sparked her interest in learning more about photography and, as a result, she decided to study photography at Columbia University. After she completed her education, she traveled for a while before settling in San Francisco. There she opened her own photography studio.

When the Great Depression began, Lange started to photograph people throughout San Francisco's neighborhoods. Some were homeless or hungry—and many had no jobs. A number of people were taking part in labor strikes.[1] She did not like what she saw in the streets. Her images of people standing in lines waiting for bread or eating in soup kitchens showed the awful conditions people had to live through.

Lange wanted to tell a story with each picture she took. For example, she saw a man standing in a breadline holding a tin cup. His back was turned away from the other people in line. His face was thin and worn. He had the look of someone who had given up all hope. Lange snapped that image.

Photographers of her era saw this photograph and many others Lange had taken. Because of this, she became known for her ability to see into the hearts and minds of her subjects. Lange showed not only the horrible outside living conditions, but also the inside struggles of the people. This was the start of her career as a documentary[2] photographer.

[1] **labor strikes**: the stopping of work to protest against poor working conditions

[2] **documentary**: presentation of actual events or facts about something

What does the author think about Lange?

What are Lange's reasons for choosing her subjects?

How did Lange work with her subjects? How did that method affect how the photographs came out?

Real Images, Real Stories

Lange's fame had spread to people in the government. Because of this, she and her husband were asked to work for the Farm Security Administration (FSA). This was one of the programs created by President Roosevelt's New Deal. Lange photographed victims of the Dust Bowl[3] and the Great Depression. Lange's husband wrote reports about their experiences.

Due to the drought and dust storms on the Great Plains, thousands of farm families had been forced to move west looking for work; they became migrant workers. Many ended up in California. However, California already had a large population of migrant workers. These people lived in rundown shacks or torn tents. They had little food or water or other necessary services. Unfortunately, conditions did not improve for those fleeing the Dust Bowl states to California.

Lange began photographing people living in these conditions. Before she took a picture, she talked to each subject because she wanted the person to be comfortable with her. With many of her photos, she included captions. Sometimes Lange wrote essays about the images she captured on camera. Her work and the work of some others helped the government realize how bad things were for migrant workers. As a result, the government provided money for California to build migrant camps for these people.

Lange continued her work photographing people and telling their stories. She focused on the people she believed were forgotten. Her goal became making the public aware of their troubles. Her photographs appeared in magazines and newspapers; they helped raise awareness about migrant workers.

[3] **Dust Bowl**: the name given to the southern Great Plains states of Texas, Oklahoma, New Mexico, Colorado, and Kansas during the dust storms of the 1930s

Reading Guide

In what way was the FSA successful? In what way was it unsuccessful?

Why was the work of Dorothea Lange and other FSA photographers important?

In 1936, Lange saw a woman sitting with her children in the middle of a deserted field. They were in a worn tent with no food or supplies. Lange took a series of photographs of this woman and her children. The woman, hungry and with no means of support, had been forced from her home in a Dust Bowl state.

People were troubled by what they saw in Lange's photographs. This caused the government to send twenty thousand pounds of food to the camp where the migrant mother was staying. Another effect was that writers and other photographers began to pay more attention to the suffering of these people and others throughout the country.

Dorothea Lange, together with many other photographers hired by the FSA, created a historical portrait of the Dust Bowl and the Great Depression. About 270,000 pictures were taken. Many of these pictures can still be seen today at the Library of Congress in Washington, D.C.

This photograph, known as "Migrant Mother," was taken in 1936 in Nipomo, California.

Answer the following questions.

1 This question has two parts. First, answer Part A. Then, answer Part B.

Part A

Read the following excerpt from "Photographing History." Underline **two** words or phrases that identify the structure used in the passage.

> **Lange began photographing people living in these conditions. Before she took a picture, she talked to each subject because she wanted the person to be comfortable with her. With many of her photos, she included captions. Sometimes Lange wrote essays about the images she captured on camera. Her work and the work of some others helped the government realize how bad things were for migrant workers. As a result, the government provided money for California to build migrant camps for these people.**

Part B

How does the overall text structure of "Photographing History" contrast with "Franklin D. Roosevelt and the New Deal"?

A. "Photographing History" has a compare-and-contrast structure; "Franklin D. Roosevelt and the New Deal" has a problem-solution structure.

B. "Photographing History" has a problem-solution structure; "Franklin D. Roosevelt and the New Deal" has a cause-and-effect structure.

C. "Photographing History" has a chronological structure; "Franklin D. Roosevelt and the New Deal" has a compare-and-contrast structure.

D. "Photographing History" has a cause-and-effect structure; "Franklin D. Roosevelt and the New Deal" has a chronological structure.

2 The authors of both "Photographing History" and "Franklin D. Roosevelt and the New Deal" discuss how the Dust Bowl affected farmers. Compare and contrast the approach each author took to relate this information.

_____

_____

_____

_____

_____

_____

_____

3 Read the following excerpt from the passage.

She focused on the people she believed were forgotten.

Which detail from the passage **best** supports this statement? Choose **all** that apply.

A. Her images of people standing in lines waiting for bread or eating in soup kitchens showed the awful conditions people had to live through.

B. Because of this, she and her husband were asked to work for the Farm Security Administration.

C. Lange continued her work photographing people and telling their stories.

D. Her photographs appeared in magazines and newspapers; they helped raise awareness about migrant workers.

E. In 1936, Lange saw a woman sitting with her children in the middle of a deserted field.

4 The following question has two parts. First, answer Part A. Then, answer Part B.

Part A

What does the term <u>migrant worker</u> mean, as it is used in the passage?

A. to wait for work to be available

B. to work in one location

C. to move regularly when looking for work

D. to work in large groups

Part B

Which excerpt from the passage supports the answer to Part A?

A. Many ended up following the harvest in California.

B. However, California already had a large population of migrant workers.

C. These people lived in run-down shacks or torn tents.

D. Unfortunately, conditions did not improve for those fleeing the Dust Bowl states to California.

5 How does Dorothea Lange's photograph "Migrant Mother" help the author make the point that Lange's photographs caused a change in people's attitudes toward the migrant workers? Cite specific details from the passage to support your answer.

_____

_____

_____

_____

6 The authors of "Franklin D. Roosevelt and the New Deal" and "Photographing History" write about a time in history when the government took a much greater role in people's lives. Compare and contrast the authors' points of view on the New Deal and the role of government programs. Be sure to include details from both passages to support your answer.

Write your answer on the lines below.

_____

_____

_____

_____

_____

_____

_____

_____

_____

_____

_____

_____

_____

_____

_____

_____

RI.5.4, RI.5.5, RI.5.6, RI.5.7, L.5.4.a, L.5.6

Scientific and Technical Texts

❶ GETTING THE IDEA

Authors of scientific and technical texts write with the **purpose**, or intention, to inform or explain. They often present information without expressing a personal **point of view**, or position on the topic. A **scientific text** explains a scientific topic, such as the life cycle of a frog or the rings of Saturn. Science magazines, science textbooks, and experiments are examples of scientific texts. **Technical texts** provide detailed information about a specific topic or how to perform a specific task. User manuals, instructions, brochures, and recipes are examples of technical texts.

Scientific and technical texts include **domain-specific vocabulary**, or words that have to do with a specialized topic. To define these words, the author may include a **glossary**, which is an alphabetical list of terms and their definitions in a book. The author may also use different techniques to define words within the text.

Define words by . . .	Example
definition	Pasteurization is a process in which milk is briefly heated to a high temperature to kill bacteria.
example	Many sailors use celestial bodies, such as the sun, moon, and the stars, to navigate.
explanation	Sauté the onions in a little oil. Keep the pan on medium heat and lightly toss or stir the onions as they cook.
footnotes	A coral reef is a habitat[1] uniquely well suited to the parrot fish. **[1]habitat:** the place where a living thing lives

Text Structure

Like most nonfiction texts, scientific and technical texts contain a lot of information. To make the information easier to understand and remember, authors organize their facts and details using various text structures. In addition to common structures, such as compare and contrast, cause and effect, and problem and solution, authors may use structures such as the ones listed below.

- A **sequential structure** presents ideas and concepts in the order in which they happen. In science and technical texts, the author may use time-order words, such as *first* and *next*, or show a process with numbered steps.

- A **general-to-specific structure** begins with a general statement or idea and then supports the statement with specific examples.

- In a **part-to-whole structure** the facts and details lead to one main idea or concept.

- A **spatial structure** describes things in terms of where they are. It uses location words such as *top*, *bottom*, *front*, *back*, *north*, and *west*. Descriptions often use a spatial structure.

Graphic Features

A **graphic feature** is an image that helps you visualize information. Some graphic features clarify the meaning of the text. Others show a lot of information in a compact way. Scientific and technical texts use a variety of graphic features to help you understand a topic.

- A **circle graph** is a drawing that shows the parts of a whole.

Weather in July

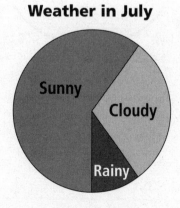

- A **model** is a picture or object that represents a much larger, real-life object. For example, a globe is a model of Earth.

- A **diagram** is a drawing that shows and labels the different parts of something.

Parts of an Insect

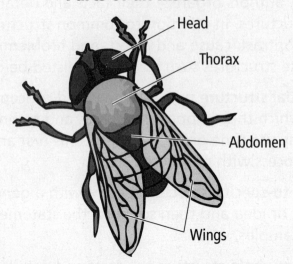

Head

Thorax

Abdomen

Wings

- A **flowchart** shows steps in a process or how things relate to one another by using arrows or connecting lines. Life cycles and food chains are often illustrated using flowcharts.

Life Cycle of a Housefly

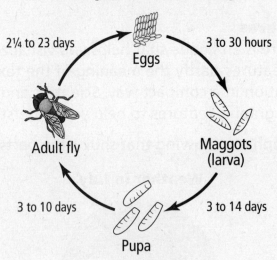

2¼ to 23 days

Eggs

3 to 30 hours

Maggots (larva)

3 to 14 days

Pupa

3 to 10 days

Adult fly

- **Bar graphs** and **line graphs** use bars or lines to compare and contrast ideas or show how ideas relate to one another.

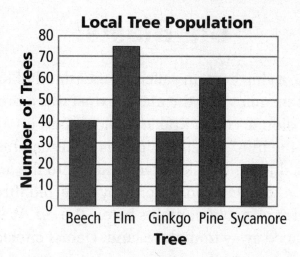

- A **table** uses columns and rows to organize information.

Time	Temperature
2:00 PM	55°F
2:15 PM	58°F
2:30 PM	59°F
2:45 PM	56°F

Language Spotlight • Academic Vocabulary

Academic vocabulary is made up of words that are traditionally used in school discussions and textbooks. Sometimes, you can use context to figure out the meaning of academic vocabulary. Read the sentences below. The underlined words are examples of academic vocabulary. What do these terms mean?

When you perform a science <u>investigation</u>, you first make a <u>hypothesis</u> in the form of a question. A hypothesis is an idea that can be tested.

What additional academic vocabulary words might you use when doing a science investigation?

Read the passage.

Big Blasts!

In May 1883, a ship captain sailed by the island of Krakatau and saw dust rising six miles into the air. The dust was a preview of an awesome explosion to come. Krakatau blew apart on August 26, 1883, in one of the most violent eruptions in human history. The first blast threw gas, dust, and rocks fifteen miles into the air. Four more blasts were heard the next morning. They occurred three thousand miles away and sank two mountains below the sea. Walls of water 120-feet high raced away from the island. Debris circled the entire globe, but the air around Krakatau was so thick with dust that the sun was not visible for three days.

What Are Volcanoes?

Volcanoes are openings in Earth's surface where magma pushes out. They take their name from *Vulcan*, the name for the Roman god of fire, because they often spit out fiery, melted rock. Not all volcanoes, however, put on a thrilling show. Many lie dormant, sitting quietly for long periods of time. Others become extinct and stop erupting completely. When a volcano is active, though, its display combines science and beauty.

Earth's surface is always in motion. Giant sheets of land and ocean, called plates, slide by one another, pushing together, and pulling apart. Openings can form at the places where plates meet. Most volcanoes exist near plate boundaries.

Beneath Earth's surface, temperatures are so high that rock melts. This melted rock, called magma, can ooze underground. Because it is less dense than the rocks around it, though, it slowly rises. When enough pressure builds at the surface, it explodes. Above the surface, magma is called lava. Besides lava, gas, rocks, ash, and dust can erupt from volcanoes.

Magma rises through cracks in rocks and pushes through to the surface, forming a volcano.

Where Do Volcanoes Form?

The world's busiest place for volcanic activity is along "The Ring of Fire" in the Pacific Ocean. Seventy-five percent of Earth's active and dormant volcanoes lie along this stretch of land and water. Here, a giant plate holding up the Pacific Ocean meets several other plates. At its borders, hundreds of volcanoes appear as a plate pushes up or slides under other plates.

There is much to learn about volcanoes. By studying Earth's estimated 1,500 active and thousands of dormant volcanoes, scientists will continue to discover how and why they form and erupt.

Answer the following questions.

1 This question has two parts. First, answer Part A. Then, answer Part B.

Part A

What is the author's purpose for writing this passage? Choose **all** that apply.

A. to explain what a volcano is

B. to persuade people to take precautions during volcanic eruptions

C. to entertain with a story about a volcanic eruption

D. to describe how and where volcanoes form

Part B

Circle **two** sentences in the passage that support the answer to Part A.

Hint Think about the purpose of science articles. Then look at the text features in the article for clues.

2 Explain why a volcano erupts. Use information from the passage and the diagram and its caption to support your response.

_____

_____

_____

_____

_____

_____

_____

_____

Hint Which section of the passage explains why volcanoes erupt? What does the diagram's caption explain about magma?

3 The following question has two parts. First, answer Part A. Then, answer Part B.

Part A

What does the word <u>dormant</u> mean?

A. exploding

B. active

C. full of action

D. in a state of rest

Part B

Which words from the passage **best** support the answer to Part A?

A. thrilling show

B. sitting quietly

C. long periods of time

D. become extinct

Hint Look at the phrases and sentences before and after *dormant*. Which choices give clues about what *dormant* means?

4 The following question has two parts. First, answer Part A. Then, answer Part B.

Part A

Read the following excerpt from the passage.

> **By studying Earth's <u>estimated</u> 1,500 active and thousands of dormant volcanoes, scientists will continue to discover how and why they form and erupt.**

What does the word <u>estimated</u> mean?

A. exactly

B. measured

C. less than

D. approximately

Part B

Write a sentence using <u>estimated</u> that supports the answer to Part A.

_____

_____

Hint The word *estimated* is often used in math to discuss numbers and amounts. How is the word used to discuss numbers in this excerpt?

Use the Reading Guide to help you understand the passage.

Lava Lab

Reading Guide

Why would scientists want to make lava in a lab rather than study it in nature?

Identify the steps needed to make lava in a lab. How does the flowchart help you understand those steps?

What are some experiments scientists have done with lava made in a lab?

Science might seem like serious business, but it can also be a lot of fun. Consider the work of Jeffrey Karson. He knew lava could be difficult to study in nature. On-site experiments with lava are challenging because volcanic eruptions cannot be planned or controlled. So, Karson and the Syracuse University Lava Project (SULP) found a solution. They made their own lava.

In order to create lava, Karson had to melt rocks. The process starts with basalt. These dull-looking rocks are ancient—more than one billion years old—and common.

Making Lava

There are several steps to making lava. First, the rocks are crushed into small pieces. Then they are put in a bathtub-sized crucible[1] and heated to over 2,200 °F for a few hours until they melt. The melted rock bubbles and splutters, looking like bright orange, boiling oatmeal.

Next, the melted rock is poured from the crucible into a track of dry sand. The lava can now be used in experiments.

Scientists and students have used homemade lava to research various questions. In one experiment, they investigated how the slope of the track affected the lava flow. In another, they used different surfaces on the bottom of the track to see how lava flowed over each one.

Steps in Making Homemade Lava

Basalt rocks are crushed. → Crushed rock goes into a crucible. → Rock is heated to 2,200°F. → Rock melts into lava. → Lava is poured into a track.

[1] **crucible**: a pot in which metals or other substances are heated to a very high temperature or melted

Reading Guide

Was SULP the only group to make lava in a lab? Explain.

How do the subheads help you understand how the text is organized?

Other than in science experiments, how can lava made in a lab be useful?

Lots of Lava

The Syracuse University Lava Project isn't the only lava project in history, but it is certainly the biggest and the most advanced. In the late 1700s, a Scottish geologist named James Hall was studying rocks. He successfully used a blacksmith's forge to melt basalt and produce a very small amount of lava. Since then, other projects have been able to make a few ounces of lava.

At Syracuse University, however, the amount of lava created is huge! The first experiments produced more than ten pounds of lava, but the amount quickly grew to hundreds of pounds. Now, the Lava Project can make a nearly continuous amount of lava, and as a result, the experiments better mimic a real lava flow. As of August 2012, the project had run over a hundred separate pours. It is the largest and most regular lava project in history, and a unique one in the world today.

Community Participation

The Lava Project experiments are held outdoors, and guests from local schools and the community are welcome to watch. Sometimes they even pitch in. In one experiment, people threw objects into the lava. Their contribution helped scientists learn how barriers affect lava flow.

Community involvement goes beyond just science. Many experiments end with everyone roasting hot dogs and marshmallows over the cooling lava. Students often take home pieces of cooled lava as souvenirs. Artists use the lava to create sculptures as large as thirty feet or more. However, to make works of art using lava, the lava must cool without cracking. Artists discovered that inserting a metal rod into the cooling lava prevents cracking. That discovery gave scientists valuable information about how lava cools under different conditions.

The Lava Project provides scientists a way to learn about lava in controlled, safe ways. It provides insight about how lava flows and cools. That information could be important the next time a volcano roars to life.

Duplicating any part of this book is prohibited by law. © 2015 Triumph Learning, LLC

Answer the following questions.

1 This question has two parts. First, answer Part A. Then, answer Part B.

Part A

Read the following excerpt from the passage.

> **These dull-looking rocks are <u>ancient</u>—more than one billion years old— and common.**

What does the word <u>ancient</u> mean?

A. ordinary

B. boring

C. recent

D. very old

Part B

Write a sentence using <u>ancient</u> that supports the answer to Part A.

_____

_____

_____

2 Read the following excerpt from the passage.

> **First, the rocks are crushed into small pieces. Then they are put in a bathtub-sized <u>crucible</u>[1] and heated to over 2,200°F for a few hours until they melt.**

What does the author do to help readers understand the meaning of the domain-specific word <u>crucible</u>?

_____

_____

_____

3 The following question has two parts. First, answer Part A. Then, answer Part B.

Part A

What is a geologist?

A. an experiment

B. a large amount of something

C. a scientist who studies Earth

D. a tool used to melt rocks

Part B

Which words from the passage **best** support the answer to Part A?

A. lava project

B. studying rocks

C. melt basalt

D. first experiments

Answer the following questions about both passages.

4 Look at the graphic feature in each passage. How does each graphic feature add to your understanding of that passage?

_____

_____

_____

_____

_____

_____

5 Read all parts of the question before responding.

Part A

What is the overall text structure of "Big Blasts!"?

A. cause and effect

B. problem and solution

C. sequence

D. general to specific

Part B

What is the overall text structure of "Lava Lab"?

A. part to whole

B. general to specific

C. sequence

D. spatial

Part C

How does each author's choice of text structure help make the information clearer? Use details from both passages to support your response.

_____

_____

_____

_____

_____

6 In what way is lava made in a lab different from lava produced during a volcanic eruption? Use details from both "Lava Lab" and "Big Blasts!" to support your response.

Write your response on the lines below.

_____

_____

_____

_____

_____

_____

_____

_____

_____

_____

_____

_____

_____

_____

Analyze Informational Texts

1 GETTING THE IDEA

Have you ever heard people refer to the "Information Age"? This phrase refers to the wealth of information available through print, digital, and multimedia sources. When you want to know more about a topic, you probably refer to more than one source. By using multiple sources, you add to your knowledge of a topic. You might check multiple nonfiction texts to:

- locate an answer to a question.

- solve a problem quickly and efficiently.

- learn more about a historical event or scientific concept.

- write or speak about a topic knowledgeably.

When you reference multiple nonfiction texts, it is important to make comparisons and connections among the sources. Let's suppose, for example, you are researching geysers. You might:

- read a section in a science textbook about how geysers form.

- read an online article about geysers around the world.

- read an essay about the threats that geothermal power plants pose to geysers.

- view a webcam of Old Faithful, a geyser in Yellowstone National Park.

Each source has geysers as its main topic; however, the text type, structure, point of view, and main ideas may be very different.

Summarizing

A good summary helps you remember what you read and shows that you understand the text. To begin, examine each source separately. Identify the main ideas and supporting details. Think about how the events or ideas connect to one another and to the topic. Look for key words and phrases that will help you discuss the topic. Then **summarize** the text by restating the main ideas and key points in your own words.

Making Comparisons

Comparing and contrasting texts helps you deepen your understanding of a topic. To compare texts, look for ways in which they are alike. To contrast texts, look for ways in which they are different. Consider each text type, its structure, and its author's point of view. Let's use geysers as an example.

- A **science textbook** entry about geysers gives a general overview of the topic. It may use a sequence structure to tell how geysers form. The author's point of view is objective, sharing only facts and details—not the author's feelings.

- An **online article** about geysers around the world may have a compare-and-contrast structure. The writing may be less formal and may address the reader directly. The author may directly share his or her feelings about the topic.

- An **essay** about the threat that geothermal plants pose to geysers may have a problem-and-solution structure. The article may contain **bias**, or a strong belief, as the author shares his or her opinion. The author may include facts that support his or her opinion.

- A **webcam** of Old Faithful will give the viewer a chance to see a geyser erupting. Viewing a webcam allows the viewer to form his or her own opinions about a topic.

Read the following passages. Underline the main idea in each, and circle the key words you need to know. How does the structure of each help you identify the main idea and the author's purpose?

Invertebrates are animals without backbones. Arthropods make up the largest group of invertebrates. An arthropod has jointed legs, a body with distinct sections, and a hard outer covering called an exoskeleton.

Some people believe spiders are insects, but this is not true. Spiders belong to a group of arthropods called arachnids. A spider's body has only two sections, but an insect's body has three. A spider has eight legs. In contrast, an insect has six legs.

Making Connections

Once you compare and contrast the texts, make connections among them in order to integrate the information. When you **integrate information**, you take the important ideas from each source to show that you have knowledge of a particular topic.

The following paragraph shows how you might integrate information from both passages above in order to share your knowledge of spiders.

> Spiders are invertebrates. They belong to a group of arthropods called arachnids. They have eight jointed legs, a body with two distinct sections, and an exoskeleton.

Language Spotlight • Transition Words and Phrases

Transitions are words or phrases that connect ideas in a text to show how they are related. Transitions can be used to show:

- similarity: *also, in the same way, just as*

- differences: *but, however, in contrast, yet, still, on the other hand*

- sequence or time: *first, second, third, next, then, finally, before, after, meanwhile*

- cause and effect: *so, therefore, consequently, because*

- emphasis: *even, in fact, of course, truly, indeed*

- an example: *for example, for instance, specifically, to illustrate, furthermore*

Reread the passage on page 123 that compares spiders and insects. Draw a box around the transition words. How do the transition words help you connect the ideas in the text?

Read the passage.

Helping Helpful Insects

What do you do when an insect buzzes around you? Do you try to swat it? Well, don't—that insect may be helpful! In fact, there are more insects that are helpful than there are harmful ones. More than one hundred thousand kinds of insects live in the United States, but fewer than 1 percent are harmful to plants or destroy crops.

So how are the other 99 percent of insects beneficial to humans? Some insects, such as bees and wasps, pollinate crops so they can produce food. Others, such as beetles and ants, break down dead or decaying plant and animal matter, which results in returning nutrients to the soil. Still others provide humans with products. Honeybees make honey and wax, and silkworms produce silk. One of the most important jobs that some beneficial insects have, however, is getting rid of harmful insects.

Beneficial insects that keep harmful insects in check can be predators or parasites. Predators eat their prey. The ladybug, for example, is a predator. Both the adult ladybug and its larvae eat harmful insects, such as aphids and mites, that destroy plants. Parasites, on the other hand, don't kill their prey. Instead, they feed on pests or use them as a nursery, laying their eggs in other insects. When the eggs hatch, the larvae feed on the host. Examples of parasites include some kinds of wasps and flies.

Although beneficial insects far outnumber harmful ones, insect pests can still damage gardens and crops. In an effort to control these pests, people often use pesticides, or poisons, to kill them. The problem with pesticides is that they kill beneficial insects along with the pests!

What can you do to help beneficial insects? Check plants carefully, especially the backs of leaves, to catch pest problems early. Instead of spraying an entire yard or garden with pesticides, spot-treat only the plants that have pests. Use less harmful pesticides or use special soaps and plant oils that help control pests without the use of poisons.

In conclusion, beneficial insects are necessary to humans and to the balance of nature. So the next time you're about to swat an insect, think twice. You may be doing more harm than good.

Answer the following questions.

1 What is the **best** summary of "Helping Helpful Insects"?

   A. Insects can be annoying when they fly or buzz around you. There are more than one hundred thousand kinds of insects in the United States. Fewer than 1 percent are harmful. The other 99 percent are beneficial.

   B. Insects are equally helpful and harmful. They eat plants but pollinate crops. Pesticides can kill both beneficial and harmful insects, so use pesticides carefully.

   C. Most insects are helpful. They pollinate crops, break down plant and animal matter, make products, and control other pests. Using too many pesticides upsets this balance of nature.

   D. Using pesticides can kill all of the insects around your house. There are other ways to kill harmful insects. Remember, beneficial insects far outnumber the harmful ones.

> **Hint** A summary includes the main ideas from a passage. Identify the main idea in each paragraph and use that information when choosing your answer.

2 Read the sentence in each choice. Then, match the underlined word in the sentence to its closest definition on the right.

A. Parasites, on the other hand, don't kill their prey.	**1.** an organism that preys on other living things
	2. an organism that lives on or in other living things
B. When the eggs hatch, the larvae feed on the host.	**3.** helpful in some way
	4. an early wormlike form of some living things
C. In an effort to control these pests, people often use pesticides, or poisons, to kill them.	**5.** poisons
	6. dead or decaying plant and animal matter

> **Hint** Look for clues in the words around an underlined word to help you determine its meaning.

3 The following question has two parts. First, answer Part A. Then, answer Part B.

Part A

Which **best** describes the text type of "Helping Helpful Insects"?

A. article

B. textbook

C. essay

D. webcam

Part B

What does the text type tell a reader about the author's point of view? Cite evidence from the passage in your response.

_____

_____

_____

Hint Remember that the structure of a passage and whether or not the author presents his or her point of view are clues to text type.

4 Which of the following **best** describes the structure of "Helping Helpful Insects"?

A. general to specific: The author states a general idea about beneficial insects and supports it with facts and details.

B. compare and contrast: The author compares beneficial and harmful insects.

C. sequential: The author tells in order what beneficial insects do.

D. part to whole: The author states details that lead up to one idea.

Hint The structure of a nonfiction text is the way in which the author organizes the information.

Use the Reading Guide to help you understand the passage.

Food for the Future

Duplicating any part of this book is prohibited by law. © 2015 Triumph Learning, LLC

Reading Guide

On which continents do people traditionally eat insects?

What does FAO stand for?

What does the graph tell you about the kinds of insects that people eat?

When students think of a healthful snack, insects don't usually come to mind. Yet throughout the world, billions of people eat insects on a regular basis. Insects are popular snacks in tropical regions and are a traditional food in many parts of Asia, Africa, and Latin America. In these places, it's not unusual to find beetles, caterpillars, bees, or ants on the menu.

The United Nations has taken an interest in insects. In 2013, its Food and Agriculture Organization (FAO) released a report about insects. The FAO report states that "more than 1,900 insects species have been documented as <u>edible</u>" and suggests that insects be explored as food for the future.

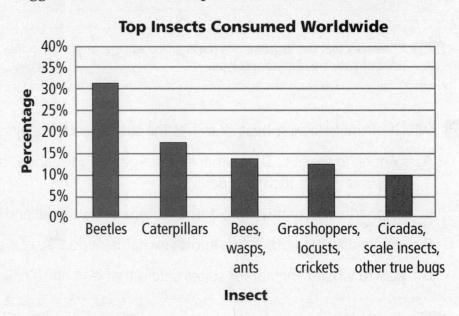

Top Insects Consumed Worldwide

Why Eat Insects?

The world's population is growing. By the year 2050, Earth will be home to nine billion people. To feed these people, food production will need to nearly double. This fact poses many questions. How will people meet their nutritional needs? Where will people find the land to grow more crops or raise livestock? How will this affect the environment? What will all this food production cost?

Reading Guide

What problems does a growing world population pose?

How does each benefit address one of these problems?

Why have Western cultures been slow to accept insects as a food source?

In short, the FAO report acknowledges that new food sources are needed and suggests that entomophagy may be an answer. *Entomophagy* is the practice of eating insects. A closer look at the benefits of eating insects supports this solution.

Health Benefits Insects can help people meet their nutritional needs. Insects are rich in protein and good fats. In addition, they are high in calcium, iron, and zinc. This makes them healthful alternatives to chicken, pork, beef, and even fish.

Environmental Benefits Raising livestock requires land for grazing and for growing animal feed. In contrast, insects require little land. They can be raised in confined places and on land unsuitable for crops.

Furthermore, insects are environmentally friendly. They produce fewer greenhouse gases than most livestock. As nature's recyclers, they also break down plant and animal waste. Since a growing world population means more waste, organic waste can be fed to insects.

Economic Benefits The cost of raising livestock is high. Animals must be cared for, watered, and fed. They also take a long time to mature. Most insects, however, require little care. They feed on organic waste and need little water. They also mature in a few weeks. Since most insects are eaten at the egg and larval stages, they are more quickly available as a food source.

Raising and harvesting insects can also give people a way to earn a living. In the wild, they are harvested at no cost. Moreover, raising insects is a low-tech business. It requires little equipment. People could easily raise them at home for personal use or to sell.

Looking to the Future

The FAO recognizes that the idea of eating insects may be strange, especially to Western countries. It suggests that eating insects never gained popularity in the West because livestock and crops met people's food demands. It further suggests that insects were viewed "as a nuisance and threat to food production."

What details show that Western cultures may eventually accept insects into their diets?

What example is given to show that people can change their attitudes toward a food?

What information can you learn from the table?

Whatever the reason, many Western cultures view insects with disgust. Western people have been slow to accept insects into their diets. However, feelings toward insects are changing. Some restaurants now have insects on the menu, and specialty food stores sell insects. Recipes for insects can even be found in some cookbooks and online.

"I don't expect it to be something that happens very quickly," says Eva Muller, one of FAO's directors. "But if we remember that twenty years ago, nobody in Europe would think of eating raw fish, and everybody now loves sushi, things can change."

Insects can be eaten whole or ground into a powder or paste and incorporated into other foods. To see how some insects are served, look at the chart below.

Insects on the Menu		
Edible Insects	**Country**	**How Prepared**
Witchetty grubs	Australia	fire-roasted
silkworm pupae	China	deep-fried
stink bugs	Indonesia	roasted
grasshoppers	Mexico	roasted, served with avocado in a tortilla
ants	Thailand	eggs and larvae canned
termites	Uganda	eaten raw from the mound
Mopane caterpillars	Botswana	stewed
crickets	United States	placed inside lollipops

CAUTION: Do not eat insects if you have a known food allergy or are allergic to pollen or dust. Not all insects are edible, and some are poisonous. It is not safe to eat an insect that is not harvested and prepared properly.

Answer the following questions.

1 Read the excerpt in each choice. Then match the underlined word in the sentence to its closest definition on the right.

A. The FAO report states that "more than 1,900 insects species have been documented as <u>edible</u>"...

B. Raising <u>livestock</u> requires land for grazing and for growing animal feed.

C. They also take a long time to <u>mature</u>.

1. animals that prey on other living things

2. animals raised as a food source

3. to grow to adulthood

4. a feeling of disgust

5. able to be eaten

6. animals that eat plants

2 What can a reader learn from the bar graph on page 128? Choose **all** that apply.

A. when certain insect species are edible worldwide

B. what kinds of insect species are eaten worldwide

C. how many of each insect species are eaten worldwide

D. where insect species live worldwide

E. how food is prepared worldwide

F. some kinds of insect species currently identified as edible

Answer the following questions about both passages.

3 Both "Helping Helpful Insects" and "Food for the Future" are about the benefits of insects. How are the authors' points of view different? Use details from both passages to support your response.

_____

_____

_____

_____

4 Consider the overall structure of "Helping Helpful Insects" and the overall structure of "Food for the Future." Then compare and contrast the two passages to tell how their structures are alike and different. Use details from each passage to support your response.

Write your answer on the lines below.

_____

_____

_____

_____

_____

5 This question has two parts. First, answer Part A. Then, answer Part B.

Part A

Read the following excerpt from "Helping Helpful Insects." Underline **three** phrases that tell how insects benefit the environment.

> **Some insects, such as bees and wasps, pollinate crops so they can produce food. Others, such as beetles and ants, break down dead or decaying plant and animal matter, which results in returning nutrients to the soil. Still others provide humans with products. Honeybees make honey and wax, and silkworms produce silk.**

Part B

What information from "Food for the Future" adds to your understanding of how insects are beneficial?

_____

_____

_____

_____

6 You have read two passages about insects, "Helping Helpful Insects" and "Food for the Future." Consider the points each author makes. Integrate the information you read to write **three** paragraphs that demonstrate your knowledge of insects and their benefits.

Write your answer on the lines below.

_____

_____

_____

_____

_____

_____

_____

_____

_____

_____

_____

_____

_____

_____

_____

_____

RI.5.9, L.5.4.a, L.5.5.c

Analyze Texts Across Genres

1 GETTING THE IDEA

Authors may present information about a single topic in many ways. For example, one author may write an informational text to give facts and details about the planet Mars. Another may write a science fiction story to tell a tale about aliens living on Mars.

Fiction or Nonfiction

Fiction is a made-up story, while **nonfiction** presents facts. However, readers can compare and contrast fiction and informational texts that are related in some way.

Fiction	Both	Nonfiction
• tells imaginative stories • includes characters, setting, and plot events • uses dialogue, description, and pacing to enhance the text	• may present information in the form of a story • are told from a particular point of view • can include scientific or historical facts	• gives facts about a topic • may be broken into sections separated by headings • includes graphic features such as diagrams, charts, and graphs

Fiction includes fables, myths, and realistic fiction. Nonfiction texts include articles, instructions, and recipes. Each type of text has unique features that readers can identify. Some text types include elements of fiction and nonfiction.

- Historical fiction and historical texts are about real people and events from the past. However, historical fiction may include made-up characters, events, and details, while historical texts stick to facts.

- Science fiction is set in the future, in space, or on another planet. Like a scientific or technical text, science fiction includes real-life details about science and technology, but it tells a story through made-up characters, events, and details.

- Literary nonfiction includes biographies, autobiographies, and memoirs. These texts tell true stories about real people. However, they often make use of storytelling techniques such as including vivid details or building suspense and conflict.

Analyze Texts

When you compare two related texts, pay close attention to the details. A fiction story may include facts from informational texts, but it will also follow a plot structure and include made-up details. In fiction, an author may take historical or scientific facts and then embellish, or exaggerate, details to make the story more interesting.

Read each passage below. One is fiction, and the other is nonfiction. Pay attention to the topic, writing style, point of view, and events in each passage. Underline any elements that are similar.

An Elephant Never Forgets

Long ago, when elephants ruled the land, the great Queen Nala reigned over both animals and people. She was a fierce and powerful ruler. Whenever she was angry, she reminded people that her massive feet could crush them to pieces. Yet one day Nala needed help. She had stepped on a spear, and it was stuck in her foot. The other animals could not help, and the people were afraid to. Finally, one brave man gently eased the spear out and patched up the wound. Nala was so grateful that she changed her attitude toward humans. Legend has it that "an elephant (and its heirs) never forgets." Generations of elephants have followed Nala's example and have developed a special bond with people.

A Special Place for Elephants

A lone baby elephant wanders along. Without a parent to protect and care for it, it may struggle to survive. But thanks to the Orphans' Project, the elephant will be rescued. The program is part of the David Sheldrick Wildlife Trust in Nairobi, Kenya. To date, the program has raised more than 150 infant elephants. When the elephants are infants, human keepers stay with them and take care of them twenty-four hours a day. Over time, the keepers help the elephants adapt and re-integrate into the wild herds.

Now let's compare and contrast the two passages.

	An Elephant Never Forgets	A Special Place for Elephants
Topic	The relationship between elephants and humans.	
Setting	thousands of years ago in Africa	modern day in Nairobi, Kenya
People/Characters	Queen Nala; a brave man	keepers at the Orphans' Project
Point of View	third-person narrative	third-person account of facts
Author's Purpose	to entertain; to offer a story that tells why "elephants never forget"	to inform about the Orphans' Project in Nairobi, Kenya

Integrate Information

Both passages have the same topic, though the information is presented differently. One told a made-up story about how elephants and people first bonded. The other informed about a real program in which humans raise elephant orphans. When you read two or more texts on the same topic, consider the information from all of the texts to form a better understanding of the topic.

- How can you use both texts to tell about elephants?

- In what other ways might the topic be presented? For example, how might a training guide for elephant keepers present information?

Language Spotlight • Synonyms and Antonyms

Synonyms are words that have the same, or almost the same, meaning. **Antonyms** are words that have opposite, or close to opposite, meanings. Identifying the relationship between pairs of synonyms and antonyms can help you understand the meaning of an unknown word. Read the paragraph below. Draw a box around a synonym and circle an antonym for the underlined word.

Just like human infants, the elephants are <u>dependent</u> on people early on. They rely on the keepers for food, affection, and comfort. They do not become independent until they are at least two years old.

Read the passage.

Dreams of a Better Future

Jamal gazed into the reflecting pool near the Lincoln Memorial. The water looked refreshing on this hot August day in 1963. Shimmering on the surface was his own face, staring back at him. It was a cute face, according to his parents, but he knew that some white people saw it as inferior. Those people weren't in the March on Washington crowd today. They were in his hometown, though. He had seen their cruel stares and heard the mean names they called him. Once, someone even threw a piece of garbage at him. So he was quiet around most white people, scared to say the wrong thing.

Jamal's best friend, Todd, was white, but Todd and his family were different from most. Jamal knew that he could always go next door and count on Todd to be there. On long summer days, the two boys would spend hours together. Usually they played baseball or went swimming in the pond. At other times, they just sat around and read comic books or watched their favorite show on television.

The boys' families were incredibly close. Their fathers even worked at the same plant doing the same job. But of course, Jamal's father made less money than Todd's father even though the only difference between the two men was the color of their skin.

This type of injustice was exactly why people had decided to have the March on Washington. The unfair conditions had gone on too long, and many people—both black and white—had grown tired of it.

Jamal and Todd were excited to be part of the tremendous crowd that had gathered for the march. They cheered, clapped, and sang along with choirs.

Then Todd's father told them that a very important man was about to speak.

"President Kennedy?" asked Todd.

"No, the president is not here. But I am sure that he will hear what this man, Dr. Martin Luther King Jr., has to say," his father replied.

Dr. King strode to the podium. He spoke of Lincoln freeing the slaves and the lack of progress since then. He spoke of a check given to African Americans but returned for insufficient funds. Jamal felt as though he were in school, learning history or economics. But then Dr. King shared his dream for the future of the country, and suddenly he had Jamal's full attention.

"I have a dream," he said, "that my four little children will one day live in a nation where they will not be judged by the color of their skin but by the content of their character."

As these words rang out over the crowd, goose bumps sprang up on Jamal's arms. He, too, dreamed of a time when his inside would matter more than what was seen on his outside. Dr. King finished his speech to thunderous applause. Standing there surrounded by the throngs of people, Jamal closed his eyes and wished that Dr. King's dream would one day come true.

Answer the following questions.

1 What genre is the passage?

A. biography

B. realistic fiction

C. historical fiction

D. newspaper article

Hint Think about the features of fiction and nonfiction, including the different genres within each. What elements of fiction and nonfiction texts does this story include?

2 The following question has two parts. First, answer Part A. Then, answer Part B.

Read the following excerpt from the passage.

> **Jamal gazed into the reflecting pool near the Lincoln Memorial. The water looked refreshing on this hot August day in 1963.**

Part A

What does the author establish in these two sentences?

A. theme

B. setting

C. author's purpose

D. conflict

Part B

Which excerpt adds more details to the answer to Part A?
Choose **all** that apply.

A. It was a cute face, according to his parents, but he knew that some white people saw it as inferior.

B. The boys' families were incredibly close.

C. This type of injustice was exactly why people had decided to have the March on Washington.

D. Jamal and Todd were excited to be part of the tremendous crowd that had gathered for the march.

E. But then Dr. King shared his dream for the future of the country, and suddenly he had Jamal's full attention.

> **Hint** For Part A, think about what you learn from the excerpt. Do you learn what the story is about, where and when it takes place, why the author wrote the story, or what the problem is? For Part B, look for sentences that give you similar information.

3 Read the sentence in each choice. Then match the underlined word in the sentence to its closest synonym on the right.

A. This type of <u>injustice</u> was exactly why people had decided to have the March on Washington.

1. appeared

B. Dr. King <u>strode</u> to the podium.

2. loud

C. As these words rang out over the crowd, goose bumps <u>sprang up</u> on Jamal's arms.

3. walked

D. Dr. King finished his speech to <u>thunderous</u> applause.

4. unfairness

4 "Dreams of a Better Future" is fiction. However, it includes real events and people, such as the March on Washington and Dr. Martin Luther King Jr. How does the inclusion of these details contribute to your understanding of the passage? Use details from the passage to support your response.

Write your answer on the lines below.

_____

_____

_____

_____

_____

_____

_____

_____

_____

_____

Use the Reading Guide to help you understand the passage.

Remembering King's Dream

Reading Guide

Notice how this passage is set up. What clues show you that this article is an informational text?

What is the author's purpose for writing this article?

Why did people organize the March on Washington in 1963?

WASHINGTON, D.C.—Thousands gathered today to celebrate the fiftieth anniversary of the March on Washington for Jobs and Freedom. That 1963 event, which drew a crowd of over two hundred thousand people, was a turning point in American history. At the height of the civil rights movement, tensions were high. African Americans were being discriminated against at work, on public buses, and at voting booths. Their basic rights were being denied.

Even though people in power were trying to address these problems, too little was actually being done. A law called the Civil Rights Act had been developed to address discrimination, but Congress had not passed it yet. People of all races were tired of the injustices that were occurring. They wanted African Americans to have the same opportunities as other American citizens. So, they decided to make their voices heard.

August 28, 1963

The March on Washington was expected to draw at least a hundred thousand people. Some people, including President Kennedy, were unsure that the march would have any impact. But their doubts were dismissed when they saw the passion displayed at the march.

People of all ages, races, and backgrounds <u>rallied</u> as one. Locking hands, they marched together and chanted. They held signs with slogans such as "We Demand Voting Rights Now." The turnout was more than double what had been expected.

How did Martin Luther King Jr. work to help the civil rights' movement?

How did Martin Luther King Jr. feel about nonviolent protests? Use the information from King's quote to help you understand his feelings.

Throughout the day, people listened to performances and speeches. Famous singers, such as Josephine Baker and Bob Dylan, sang to the crowd. Civil rights leaders and politicians gave moving speeches about the need for change. The most memorable and celebrated speech of the day was given by Reverend Dr. Martin Luther King Jr.

A Voice for Civil Rights

Growing up in Georgia, King watched his father fight against discrimination. His father believed it was wrong to mistreat people of a different race or class. His example had a major impact on King.

After graduating from Crozer Theological Seminary, King earned his doctorate from Boston University in 1955. At the time, he was only twenty-five years old. Later that year, King took on his first major role in the civil rights movement. Rosa Parks was arrested for refusing to give up her seat on a public bus. King led a bus boycott in protest, and the boycott received much attention. In the years after this, King traveled across America and gave speeches about civil rights issues.

He became known for his eloquent speech as well as for his nonviolent means of protest. Despite the countless threats targeted at him, King refused to respond with violence. After being wrongly arrested during a protest, King commented on his approach from jail. He said that nonviolent action aims to "foster such a tension that a community . . . is forced to confront the issue."

Writing Guide

What did King talk about in his "I Have a Dream" speech?

According to the author, what do people today think of King's speech?

Why do you think the author mentions that there is now a Martin Luther King Jr. Memorial in Washington, D.C.?

A Speech to Remember

Soon, these words would come true. For after the March on Washington, the issue of civil rights could no longer be ignored. King's speech on that day was the highlight of the event. He began the speech by reminding people of the past. It had been one hundred years since President Lincoln had signed the Emancipation Proclamation. And yet, African Americans were still not equal citizens. The founding fathers had written a check to all Americans when they wrote the Constitution and Declaration of Independence. The check was for "rights of life, liberty, and the pursuit of happiness." But the check the African Americans received had been returned for lack of funds.

However, King and other civil rights leaders still had hope for change. Most famously, King claimed, "I have a dream that my four little children will one day live in a nation where they will not be judged by the color of their skin but by the content of their character." He imagined a day when children of all backgrounds could hold hands and join together as sisters and brothers.

The speech became known as the "I Have a Dream" speech. Fifty years later, it is still considered one of the most powerful speeches of all time. People at today's anniversary event quoted and recited parts of the speech. Many of them were not even alive when King gave his speech. Yet, as they walked past the Martin Luther King Jr. Memorial that now stands in the city, they said thank you to King for sharing his dream with America.

Answer the following questions.

1 How do you know this passage is a work of nonfiction? Choose **all** that apply.

A. The author's purpose is to persuade the reader.

B. The author presents facts about a real event.

C. The events take place in the future.

D. The characters are made up by the author.

E. The author's purpose is to inform the audience.

F. The passage is entertaining.

2 The following question has two parts. First, answer Part A. Then, answer Part B.

Part A

Read the following excerpt from the passage.

People of all ages, races, and backgrounds <u>rallied</u> as one.

Which word is a synonym for the word <u>rallied</u>? Choose **all** that apply.

A. joined

B. separated

C. sang

D. gathered

E. walked

Part B

Which excerpt from the passage shows the meaning of the word <u>rallied</u>?

A. People of all races were tired of the injustices that were occurring.

B. Locking hands, they marched together and chanted.

C. Rosa Parks was arrested for refusing to give up her seat on a public bus.

D. However, King and other civil rights' leaders still had hope for change.

E. Many of them were not even alive when King gave his speech.

Answer the following questions about both passages.

3 This question has two parts. First, answer Part A. Then, answer Part B.

Part A

Read the excerpt from "Dreams of a Better Future" below. Underline **three** phrases that show Jamal's reaction to Dr. King's speech.

> **As these words rang out over the crowd, goose bumps sprang up on Jamal's arms. He, too, dreamed of a time when his inside would matter more than what was seen on his outside. Dr. King finished his speech to thunderous applause. Standing there surrounded by the throngs of people, Jamal closed his eyes and wished that Dr. King's dream would one day come true.**

Part B

What details from "Remembering King's Dream" add to your understanding of how people responded to the "I Have a Dream" speech?

_____

_____

_____

4 What conclusion can you make based on your reading of "Dreams of a Better Future" and "Remembering King's Dream"?

A. Jamal returned to Washington to celebrate the fiftieth anniversary of the March on Washington.

B. Martin Luther King Jr. was viewed as an important leader of the civil rights movement.

C. Martin Luther King Jr. did not influence the civil rights movement.

D. The Civil Rights Act was passed by Congress.

5 The box below contains ideas from "Dreams of a Better Future" and "Remembering King's Dream." Sort the ideas from the box into the correct columns in the chart.

African Americans, such as Jamal's dad, were paid less to do the same jobs as white people.

People wanted equal rights for African Americans.

African Americans were denied basic rights, such as the right to vote.

People wanted to protest the unfair treatment of African Americans.

Reasons for the March on Washington		
"Dreams of a Better Future"	Both	"Remembering King's Dream"

6 Both "Dreams of a Better Future" and "Remembering King's Dream" provide information about The March on Washington for Jobs and Freedom that took place on August 28, 1963. What events led up to the march? How did the march and the speech by Dr. Martin Luther King Jr. affect the people there? Use details from both passages to support your response.

Write your answer on the lines below.

_____

_____

_____

_____

_____

_____

_____

_____

_____

_____

_____

_____

_____

Read the passage.

The Great Pyramids of Tikal

Deep in the lush rainforests of northern Guatemala are the remnants of a civilization that flourished for 1,600 years. These buildings form the archeological site known as Tikal. The largest and most studied of Maya ruins, Tikal covers an area of 222 square miles. In ancient times this city was surrounded by miles of cornfields, but it was later engulfed by jungle. Tikal was rediscovered by explorers in 1848, when symmetrical hills were noticed on the rainforest floor and uncovered. At this time, only 15 percent of the ruin has been excavated.

Importance to the Maya

Tikal was a site for ceremonies that were important to the Maya, the ancestors of many people who live in Central America today. Tikal contains palaces, temples, cemeteries, and public squares. Researchers think that up to ninety thousand people made their homes in Tikal. Within the site there are at least three thousand buildings, and outside are the ruins of even more homes, mostly <u>unexcavated</u>.

Structure of the Pyramids

The pyramids of Tikal are some of the tallest structures built in the ancient Western Hemisphere. They all have a stepped shape. Some of the pyramids are short and squat, while others are quite tall. Each of the pyramids is solid, apart from tiny rooms at the top where ceremonies were held. At their bases, some contain burial chambers for the rulers who built them.

The temples in the Great Plaza were built of massive blocks of limestone and were constructed without the use of the wheel or block and tackle.[1] The buildings at Tikal are connected by paths known as causeways. The causeways were made of crushed limestone. This rock was smoothed with plaster. A similar material, stucco, was used to cover many buildings.

[1] **block and tackle** a device made with ropes and pulleys used to lift heavy materials

The Great Plaza contains six temples. Temple I, the Great Pyramid of the Jaguar, has a base that measures ten thousand square feet. Temple V is the most recently unearthed temple. It is still surrounded by the trees and vines of the rainforest. It is partially covered by vegetation. It stands 150 feet tall. Temple IV is the tallest pyramid in this group. At 212 feet, it is as tall as some of Egypt's larger pyramids. It is also known for its hieroglyphics. This temple has more of this type of writing than any other Maya location. These picture words tell the history of the families who ruled Tikal.

ceremonial rooms

In this photograph of Tikal Temple I, you can see the rooms at its top where ceremonies were held.

Tikal and the Calendar

The buildings of Tikal were used to show the changes in the year. Different buildings of Tikal line up precisely with north, south, east, and west. That is important during the equinoxes, the two days of the year when the length of day equals the length of night. On those days a person facing Temple I will see the sun rise directly over it. Similarly, a person facing Temple III will see the sun set directly behind it. On August 13, a day the ancient Maya celebrated as the birthday of the world, the sun's movement can also be noted. On that day, a person standing atop Temple I will see the sun set directly behind Temple IV.

Modern-Day Use

Tikal is visited each year by tourists from around the world. It is Guatemala's most popular tourist attraction. It has been named a World Heritage Site. That is because its buildings are evidence of a great civilization. It is also because much of the surrounding wildlife is threatened with extinction. But to some Guatemalans, the temples have another value. Since 1996, many Maya have used the site for religious events. Ceremonies mark the changes in the seasons, just as they did in times of long ago.

Answer the following questions.

1 Read all parts of the question before responding.

Part A

Which of the following sentences **best** describes a central idea developed in the passage?

A Some Maya rulers are buried in the pyramids.

B. Stucco covers many ruins in Tikal.

C. Tikal contains many ancient buildings.

D. Researchers study Tikal to learn about modern civilizations.

Part B

Write **two** details from the passage that support the idea you chose in Part A.

_____

_____

Part C

In your own words, write a brief summary that tells what the passage is about. Write your answer on the lines provided.

_____

_____

_____

_____

_____

_____

_____

_____

2 This question has two parts. First, answer Part A. Then, answer Part B.

Part A

What does the word <u>unexcavated</u> mean as it is used in the passage?

   A. outside of a cavern

   B. relating to digging

   C. relating to caves

   D. not dug up

Part B

Which pair of affixes helps you understand the meaning of <u>unexcavated</u>?

   A. the prefix *uni-* meaning "one" and the prefix *ex-* meaning "out of"

   B. the prefix *un-* meaning "not" and the suffix *-ate* meaning "to become"

   C. the prefix *ex-* meaning "out of" and the suffix *-cava* meaning "a hollow place"

   D. the prefix *cava-* meaning "a hollow place" and the suffix *-ate* meaning "to become"

3 This question has two parts. First, answer Part A. Then, answer Part B.

Part A

Which of the following text features is used to organize information in the passage?

   A. caption   **C.** heading

   B. footnote   **D.** label

Part B

On the lines below, explain how the text feature you chose in Part A helps you find information quickly. Cite an example from the passage in your answer.

_____

_____

_____

_____

4 This question has two parts. First, answer Part A. Then, answer Part B.

Part A

Match each question on the left to the section of the passage in which you would **most** likely find the answer.

A. Why is Tikal today considered a World Heritage Site?

B. Why was August 13 important to the Maya?

C. What is the difference in size between Temple IV and Temple V?

1. Importance to the Maya

2. Structure of the Pyramids

3. Tikal and the Calendar

4. Modern-Day Use

Part B

Choose one of the questions in Part A. Use details from the passage to answer it.

_____

_____

_____

5 Which evidence from the passage expresses the **most** likely cause for the fact that only 15 percent of the Tikal ruins have been excavated?

A. Tikal is visited each year by tourists from around the world.

B. Since 1996, many Maya have used the site for religious events.

C. It is also because much of the surrounding wildlife is threatened with extinction.

D. It is Guatemala's most popular tourist attraction.

Read the passage.

The Lost City

Have you ever dreamed of trekking through the jungle to find an ancient, abandoned city? This dream came true for me in Guatemala. I recently visited El Mirador, a city of many <u>superlatives</u>. It contains the world's earliest highway system and its biggest pyramid. It is one of the oldest Maya cities, and many consider it to be the cradle of Maya civilization. Surprisingly, El Mirador is not as well known as other Maya ruins. However, this may soon be changing.

The Journey

I was excited to be making the journey to El Mirador, but I found that getting there was not so easy. In contrast to other ruins, El Mirador is not yet linked into Guatemala's modern system of highways. It is thirty-seven miles from the nearest road. The site can be reached by helicopter, by horse, or even by foot. Because the site is so remote, only a few thousand people visit each year.

I hiked through the rainforest with a guide from the town of Carmelita. I needed help, as some of the rainforest plants are toxic. There are also poisonous snakes and spiders that must be avoided. And of course, I did not want to get lost.

The Causeways

Our journey continued on a road built two thousand years ago. Although this trail is ancient and crumbled, it is still useful. The *sacbe*, or white causeway, is a seven-mile road that is sixty-five to one hundred and thirty feet wide and raised up to eighteen feet off the ground. Originally it was covered in plaster and connected El Mirador to the ancient city of Nakbe. Another sacbe links El Mirador to a ruin more than twelve miles away. Some consider these joined roads to be the world's first highway system.

Our group was glad to use the sacbe instead of trekking over uneven ground. After two and a half days—and with blistered feet—we arrived at the magnificent ruin.

The Pyramids

We came upon the pyramids of El Mirador suddenly because they are half covered with trees. But when I looked closely, I could see that the buildings are stepped and grouped into sets of three. The groups rest on a platform. Our guide pointed out that the platform is the size of eighteen football fields. At 230 feet, La Danta is one of the tallest structures of the ancient world. It is also the largest. La Danta takes up more space than Egypt's largest pyramid. Like other Maya buildings, these pyramids were once decorated with a covering of painted stucco.

Unlike other archaeological sites in Guatemala, most of El Mirador has not been well excavated. Even the visible buildings are partially covered by vegetation. That makes this ancient city a very wild place. Because the buildings are so old, many of them are crumbling and require protection from rain and sun. We learned that many excavations have been filled in with soil. They will be unearthed when there is money to protect them.

The Wildlife

I was surprised by the noise of the rainforest. Although our group was quiet, the animals around us were not. We saw and heard howler monkeys and spotted many toucans and parrots. El Mirador is surrounded by an abundance of plants, such as orchids, as well as hundreds of tree species. More than three hundred more species of animals can be found in the area. At least 183 species of birds are found in the forest around El Mirador, and the area is a stopping place for birds migrating from North America.

Most visitors come to El Mirador during the dry season. So did I. Although it did not rain much during our visit, it was still hot and humid. Temperatures of more than ninety-eight degrees Fahrenheit are common year round, and for half of the year rains come daily. This makes a perfect environment for many insects. The group saw huge globe-like nests hanging from trees. Our guide identified them as termite homes. More than once, we saw leaf-cutter ants march across the forest floor.

The Future

My time at El Mirador was too short. I will certainly come back again. A trip to El Mirador is a once-in-a-lifetime journey that should be experienced by more people. The government of Guatemala agrees. They plan to turn the ruin into a tourist attraction and are considering ways to make it easier for visitors to reach. Other groups hope to turn the surrounding rainforest into a wildlife sanctuary. This will attract more tourists, and jobs for local people will result. With careful planning, the wild beauty of El Mirador will remain for all to see.

Answer the following questions.

6 This question has two parts. First, answer Part A. Then, answer Part B.

Part A

Read this excerpt from the passage.

> **Have you ever dreamed of trekking through the jungle to find an ancient, abandoned city? This dream came true for me in Guatemala. I recently visited El Mirador, a city of many <u>superlatives</u>. It contains the world's earliest highway system and its biggest pyramid. It is one of the oldest Maya cities, and many consider it to be the cradle of Maya civilization.**

Which phrase **best** describes the word <u>superlatives</u> as it is used in the excerpt?

A. better than anything else

C. worthy of praise

B. of the highest degree in a category

D. densely populated

Part B

Circle **three** details that help you understand the meaning of <u>superlatives</u>.

7 This question has two parts. First, answer Part A. Then, answer Part B.

Part A

Circle the sentence that **best** describes the author's point of view in "The Lost City."

More people should visit El Mirador.
El Mirador should be connected to a highway.
More money should be available for excavation at El Mirador.
The forest surrounding El Mirador should be protected.

Part B

Compare and contrast this point of view with the point of view taken in "The Great Pyramids of Tikal."

_____

_____

_____

8 This question has two parts. First, answer Part A. Then, answer Part B.

Part A

Four text structures are listed below. Circle the one that **best** describes the structure of "The Lost City."

Text Structures	
general to specific	chronological
part to whole	compare and contrast

Part B

Using text evidence, compare and contrast the structure of "The Lost City" with that of "The Great Pyramids of Tikal."

_____

_____

_____

_____

9 Describe the author's purpose for writing "The Lost City." How does it compare to the author's purpose for writing "The Great Pyramids of Tikal"? Remember to use textual evidence to support your ideas.

Write your answer on the lines below.

_____

_____

_____

_____

_____

PERFORMANCE TASK

You have read about Maya ruins in two texts, "The Great Pyramid of Tikal" and "The Lost City." Imagine that you are creating a brochure for people considering a trip to a Maya city. Choose three characteristics of Maya ruins you learned from the passages and describe why they might interest a visitor. Include details from both passages to support your ideas.

Write your answer on the lines below.

STRAND
3

Writing

W.5.1.a–d, W.5.2.a–c, W.5.2.e, W.5.3.a, W.5.3.c, W.5.3.e,
W.5.4, W.5.5, L.5.1.a, L.5.1.e

Writing Foundations

In school, you may be asked to write different kinds of texts—stories, reports, opinions. Regardless of what you write, you need to follow certain steps to get a final piece that is the best it can be. The steps you take make up the **writing process**. These steps include prewriting, drafting, revising, editing, and publishing.

Prewriting

Prewriting is the process of deciding on a topic and what you want to say about it. Use a graphic organizer or an outline to gather and arrange ideas. Look at the web. Underline the topic. Where would you add *blizzard*?

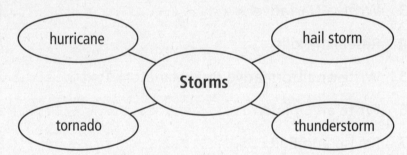

Prewriting also includes deciding on your audience and purpose. Your **audience** is your reader. In a test situation, your audience is probably your teacher. The **purpose**, or the reason for your writing, is determined by the prompt. Your purpose may be to:

- **narrate**, or tell a story about your topic.

- **inform**, or give readers facts about your topic.

- **persuade**, or convince your audience to think a certain way about your topic.

It's important to keep your audience and purpose in mind and match your style, language, and word choice accordingly. For example, story dialogue may use informal language. The language in a report should be more formal.

Once you have a good topic to write about, begin planning how you will organize your ideas in your writing. When writing a narrative, plan what happens at the beginning, middle, and end of the story.

Narrative Organization		
Beginning	**Middle**	**End**
Introduce the characters, setting, and problem or desired goal.	Describe what the characters do to solve the problem or reach the goal.	Show how the characters finally face the problem or reach the goal. Then conclude the story.

Nonfiction writing also has three main parts: an introduction, a body, and a conclusion. Use this outline to help you organize an essay, report, or opinion piece.

Introduction	State the main idea or claim you will be making about the topic.
Body	Reason 1 • Supporting detail 1 • Supporting detail 2 Reason 2 • Supporting detail 1 • Supporting detail 2
Conclusion	Summarize the most important points and leave the reader with something to think about.

Drafting

Drafting is the process of getting your ideas down on paper. In the first draft of your writing, you will probably have errors. That's OK. You can fix them in later drafts.

Revising and Editing

Revising is the process of improving your writing. This includes adding more facts or details where they are needed and deleting unrelated or repeated information. It's also a time to make sure you have used **transitions**—words and phrases that connect ideas—to make your writing flow.

Editing refers to correcting mistakes in spelling, grammar, capitalization, and punctuation. Use the following questions as a guide when you revise and edit.

- ☐ Does my response answer all parts of the prompt?
- ☐ Do I use enough relevant details?
- ☐ Are my ideas presented clearly and in a logical order?
- ☐ Is my writing style appropriate for my purpose and audience?
- ☐ Is my writing free of errors in grammar, mechanics, and spelling?

Publishing

When you **publish**, you make a clean copy of your writing for your audience. Be sure to read through your work to make any final changes before submitting it to your teacher or readers.

Language Spotlight • Conjunctions and Interjections

A **conjunction** is a word, such as *and*, *or*, *but*, or *so*, that joins other words or groups of words. Read the following sentence. The underlined word is a conjunction. What two ideas does it connect?

The wind howled, <u>and</u> the rain pummeled the windows.

An **interjection** is a word or phrase that expresses strong emotion. It is often set as its own sentence. The underlined phrase below is an interjection. What emotion does it express?

<u>Oh, no!</u> Hurricanes can be scary.

Read the passage.

Before the Storm

Hurrying upstairs, Mom knocked quickly on Jake and Jared's bedroom door. "Time to get up," she said. "We're under a hurricane watch, so wear your rain boots and slickers." Mom ignored the groans coming from the boys' room as she returned to the kitchen to finish packing lunches and preparing breakfast.

A few minutes later, Jake and Jared appeared at the breakfast table dressed for school and carrying rain boots.

"Hey! My rain boots don't fit anymore," Jake complained.

"Well," said Mom, "for now, wear your hiking boots. You need sturdy shoes."

"What's up with the hurricane?" Jared asked. "I thought it was supposed to pass us."

"You know how unpredictable hurricanes are. This one looks like it might head our way after all. But until we know more, schools and businesses are open as usual."

After Jared and Jake cleaned up their breakfast dishes, Jake ran upstairs to get his hiking boots. Then he and Jared picked up their backpacks and left for the school bus stop.

Several hours later, Mom and Dad pulled into the driveway as the school bus dropped off Jake and Jared. The hurricane watch had become a hurricane warning, so schools closed early, as well as Mom and Dad's offices. Then the family went into action. They knew the routine because they had practiced it before.

Jake and Dad pulled down and secured the hurricane shutters while Jared and Mom moved the lawn furniture and trashcans into the garage. Dad checked the emergency generator to make sure it had gasoline and was working in case the power went out. The boys put fresh batteries in the flashlights and weather radio. They already had three days' worth of food and water on hand along with a first-aid kit and emergency supplies. Furthermore, they had weekend bags packed in case they needed to evacuate and wait out the storm at Grandma's house.

When their preparations were complete, the family gathered around the television, watching the progress of the hurricane and waiting to see if they would have to evacuate.

When the storm finally hit, the winds rattled the hurricane shutters. Rain pelted the roof. The sounds were scary, but the family remained calm because they knew they had prepared well. After the power went out, they used their flashlights and listened to the weather radio. After several hours, the hurricane passed. Eventually, when it was safe to do so, the family went outdoors to inspect the damage. There were many downed tree branches and large pools of water on the lawn, but the house was OK. All in all, the damage wasn't bad. And their preparations had kept their family safe.

Answer the following questions.

1 Write the interjection from the passage and explain its function.

_____

_____

_____

_____

> **Hint** Look for a word or phrase that is abrupt or shows strong emotion. Why does the author use this word?

2 What was the author's purpose for writing this passage?

A. to argue for the importance of evacuating before a hurricane

B. to entertain with a humorous story

C. to describe the effects of a hurricane

D. to narrate events that happened in a hurricane

> **Hint** Think about what you learned from the story. How does this relate to the author's purpose?

3 This question has two parts. First, answer Part A. Then, answer Part B.

Part A

Which statement **best** describes the main idea of "Before the Storm"?

A. Jake needs new rain boots, but his hiking boots are good and sturdy.

B. Hurricanes have high winds and heavy rains.

C. Being prepared is the best way to handle a hurricane.

D. It's better to use flashlights than candles in a power outage.

Part B

Which excerpt from the passage **best** supports the answer to Part A?

A. "Hey! My rain boots don't fit any more," Jake complained.

B. . . .the winds rattled the hurricane shutters. Rain pelted the roof.

C. "You know how unpredictable hurricanes are. This one looks like it might head our way after all."

D. Then the family went into action. They knew the routine because they had practiced it before.

Hint This question asks you to do two things. Part A asks you to identify the main idea of the story. Think about how the events are related to answer Part B.

4 The following events are from the passage. In each box, write the number 2, 3, or 4 so that the events are in the correct order.

1	The family takes special preparations to get ready for the day because there is a hurricane watch.
	After the storm, the family inspects the damage outside.
	The storm hits and the power goes out, but the family is safe.
	The hurricane watch is now a warning, so the family makes additional preparations and waits for the storm.

Hint What happens in the beginning, middle, and end? Look for transitions that give hints about the sequence of events.

Use the Reading Guide to help you understand the passage.

Hurricane Hunters

Reading Guide

Why is the work of the Hurricane Hunters important?

What kinds of things do Hurricane Hunters do? Look for specific details.

Why has the author written this passage? How do you know?

Nothing can stop hurricanes, but people can do a lot to prevent loss of life and property that results from them. They can protect their homes and leave dangerous areas if they know where and when hurricanes will occur. That's where the Hurricane Hunters come in.

Tracking hurricanes is the job of the Hurricane Hunters. The Hurricane Hunters are teams of pilots and scientists who fly into storms that threaten the United States. Officially they are known as the 53rd Weather Reconnaissance Squadron. The squadron is part of the U.S. Air Force and Department of Defense.

Ready for Action

The Hurricane Hunters have to be ready to fly into storms twenty-four hours a day. In addition, they must be equipped to fly into up to three storms per flight. That is why the Hurricane Hunters have twenty flight crews.

Each flight crew has five members. They include a pilot, co-pilot, navigator, weather officer, and loadmaster. The pilot and co-pilot fly the plane. They also make sure the crew members do their jobs to complete the mission safely. The navigator prepares the flight plan and keeps an eye on the fuel gauge. The weather officer monitors atmospheric data and sends it to the National Hurricane Center. The loadmaster makes sure that all equipment is loaded and secured. He or she monitors the engines and operating systems.

The Hurricane Hunters fly a special plane to break through tropical storms. This plane has two more fuel tanks than a regular plane. The interior of the plane can be customized. The crew can set it up with whatever equipment and special instruments the mission requires.

Reading Guide

What instruments help the Hurricane Hunters gather information?

How do transition words help connect ideas in this passage?

In a "Fix"

When a storm begins to form over a body of water, the Hurricane Hunters investigate. They fly above the water at an average altitude of one thousand feet. That is about as high as a hundred-story building. The weather officer uses instruments to find the direction and speed of the winds. If he or she spots a circular motion, the mission becomes a "fix." In a "fix" mission, the crew ascends and flies into the center of the storm to get a good view.

The Hurricane Hunters fly up and enter a major hurricane at ten thousand feet. After reaching the eye, or center, of the hurricane, the weather officer releases two dropsondes. A dropsonde is a sixteen-inch tube packed with weather instruments. A tiny ten-inch parachute is attached to the top. As the dropsondes fall toward Earth, they continuously collect weather data. This data includes wind direction and speed, pressure, temperature, and humidity. The data shows what the hurricane is like from top to bottom.

Other Missions

Even when hurricanes are not raging, the Hurricane Hunters are busy dropping weather instruments from planes. For example, days before a hurricane hits, the Hurricane Hunters may drop weather buoys into bodies of water. When a weather buoy hits the water, it floats. Then its instruments begin collecting data on the approaching storm. In the winter there are few hurricanes. Even so, Hurricane Hunters drop dropsondes from as high in the atmosphere as possible. The data that these dropsondes collect is a huge help in making weather forecasts more accurate.

Worth the Danger

Hurricane Hunter pilots face a daunting and dangerous task. They have to do what pilots are trained *not* to do: fly into storms. Why? Since the Hurricane Hunters began in 1944, the data they have collected has become critical to predicting hurricanes.

The impact of the Hurricane Hunters' data is dramatic. Thanks to their data, the accuracy of hurricane forecasts has improved by 30 percent. This means that the forecasts are often right. People have come to trust these forecasts. So when the word comes to evacuate, people listen. They leave and go to safer places. This saves many lives—all thanks to the Hurricane Hunters.

Answer the following questions.

1 This question has two parts. First, answer Part A. Then, answer Part B.

Part A

Which excerpt from the passage **best** expresses the main idea of "Hurricane Hunters"?

A. The Hurricane Hunters fly a special plane to break through tropical storms. This plane has two more fuel tanks than a regular plane.

B. Tracking hurricanes is the job of the Hurricane Hunters.

C. When a storm begins to form over a body of water, the Hurricane Hunters investigate.

D. Hurricane Hunter pilots face a daunting and dangerous task. They have to do what pilots are trained *not* to do: fly into storms.

Part B

Which excerpt from the passage supports the answer to Part A? Choose **all** that apply.

A. In a "fix" mission, the crew flies into the center of the storm to get a good view.

B. Even when hurricanes are not raging, the Hurricane Hunters are busy dropping weather instruments from planes.

C. Since the Hurricane Hunters began in 1944, the data they have collected has become critical to predicting hurricanes.

D. [People] leave and go to safer places. This saves many lives—all thanks to the Hurricane Hunters.

2 Reread paragraph 1 of the passage. Circle **two** conjunctions in the paragraph that help connect ideas.

3 What was the author's **main** purpose for writing this passage?

  A. to describe what it is like to fly into a hurricane

  B. to argue for additional funding for the Hurricane Hunters

  C. to entertain with an exciting story about hunting hurricanes

  D. to explain why the work of the Hurricane Hunters is important

4 Read the following paragraph from the passage.

> **(1) The Hurricane Hunters fly a special plane to break through tropical storms. (2) This plane has two more fuel tanks than a regular plane. (3) The interior of the plane can be customized. (4) The crew can set it up with whatever equipment and special instruments the mission requires.**

The writer wants to add the following fact to the paragraph.

The extra fuel allows the plane to fly farther in one mission.

Where in the paragraph is the **best** place to add this sentence?

  A. after sentence 1

  B. after sentence 2

  C. after sentence 3

  D. after sentence 4

5 In "Before the Storm," you read about a family that takes precautions to stay safe during a hurricane. In "Hurricane Hunters," you read about what Hurricane Hunters do. Write an essay analyzing whether the work of Hurricane Hunters is important. Use reasons, facts, and details from both "Before the Storm" and "Hurricane Hunters" to support your position.

Plan your writing in the space below. Write your response on the following pages.

Plan

Write your response on the lines below.

W.5.1.a–d, W.5.9.a, L.5.1.a

Write a Response to Literature

When you write a **response to literature**, you state a position or main idea about some aspect of a story, play, or poem you have read. You base your position on an analysis of and reflection on a piece of literature, which you support with evidence from the text.

Understanding a Prompt

In class, you will often be asked to respond to a writing prompt. The prompt may ask you to respond to a text you read. Read this example. Circle the title of the poem you will analyze. Then underline the verb in the prompt.

> Explain the meaning and importance of the metaphor in Carl Sandburg's poem "Fog."

You should have circled *"Fog"* and underlined the word *Explain*. The verb in the prompt tells you what you will do: Explain an element in the poem.

Now reread the prompt. You can break it down into sections in order to understand exactly what you have to do.

- What is a metaphor?
- What is the metaphor in "Fog"?
- How does this metaphor help the reader understand the poem?

Your written response should include answers to all of these questions.

Forming Your Position

In the prompt above, you have to explain the meaning and importance of the metaphor in the poem. So, what do you think the metaphor means? Why is it important? What makes you think so? Your position is your answer to these questions.

Organizing Your Ideas

Thinking about your reasons and evidence will help you organize your ideas before you write. List the strongest reasons first. Usually the strongest reasons are the ones you can back up with facts and details from the text. For example, you can include a description of a specific event in a plot or quote a line from a poem. Also, think about how much you have to say about each reason. If you can easily write a paragraph about one of your reasons, it is likely a strong one.

Using a graphic organizer is a good way to plan and organize your ideas.

Position	In "Fog," Carl Sandburg uses a cat as a metaphor for fog, which allows the reader to visualize fog in a new, interesting way.	
Reason 1	Sandburg gives the fog cat qualities.	
Supporting details		• The fog has "little cat feet."
		• The fog sits "on silent haunches."
Reason 2	The unique comparison helps the reader visualize the fog.	
Supporting details		• People sometimes see both fog and cats as mysterious.
		• The comparison makes sense.
Conclusion	The entire poem "Fog" is a metaphor, creating an image of fog behaving like a cat.	

Developing Your Response

Use the graphic organizer as a guide for your writing. First, introduce the text you are analyzing and state your position. The introduction is a preview of the rest of your response. It reveals your purpose for writing and tells your readers what to expect.

Once you have stated your position, you need to support it. When you support a position, you give reasons to explain why you think the way you do. You also provide facts and details from the text to back up your reasons. Be sure to return to the text often while you write to confirm that you are using solid and accurate evidence.

A key to writing a good response to literature is to make sure your opinions are clearly linked to your reasons. The best way to do this is to use **transitions**, or connecting words, such as *because*, *therefore*, and *however*. Using transitions also ensures that your writing flows smoothly from one idea to the next.

The last paragraph of your writing is the conclusion. The conclusion restates your position and summarizes the most important ideas in your writing. It also often gives the reader something to think about.

Finishing Up

Reread your writing to make sure your position is clear and your reasons are logically organized and well-supported with details from the text. Proofread your work for errors in grammar, mechanics, and spelling. Make any changes needed.

Use the following checklist to guide your revision.

☐ Does my response answer all parts of the prompt?

☐ Is my position clearly stated?

☐ Is my response well-organized and focused?

☐ Do I use enough text details to support my main idea?

☐ Is my writing free of errors in grammar and mechanics?

Language Spotlight • Prepositions

Prepositions are words such as *on*, *through*, *about*, and *to*, that relate a noun or pronoun to another word in the sentence. Most prepositions tell "where" or "when" about the noun or pronoun. Read the sentences below. Underline the prepositions.

This book tells about a quest.

Greta raced across the field to score the goal.

How do the prepositions connect the phrases in the sentences?

Read the passage.

a retelling of

The Second Voyage of Sinbad the Sailor

from The Arabian Nights

After months of sailing stormy seas, I was home, and I planned to stay for a long time, living off gold from my first voyage. My last trip had been dangerous enough.

But I soon grew bored and longed for adventure. I set sail with a brave, trustworthy crew, and for months we traveled the ocean. Our last stop was an island of tall trees, their branches heavy with fruit. We hiked all day, exploring. Tired, I stopped for a nap, as my crew went on to gather fruit. I don't know how long I slept, but when I awoke, my ship and crew were gone. I cried out in despair, sure I was stranded forever.

But no challenge was unsolvable, and despair would do no good. I climbed a nearby tree, but saw only sky and water. Then a shadow fell over me; above was an enormous bird. I had heard tales of this creature, but had never seen it.

In its wings, I saw an opportunity. When it landed, I used my scarf to tie myself to its foot. We rose into the air—what a thrill it was to fly through the sky! We soon landed on another island. I untied myself and fell to the ground. Through blurry eyes, I saw the bird devouring a giant serpent. As it flew away, I looked around, realizing with dismay that I was still stranded, just on a different island.

I lay between mountains, in a valley of sparkling diamonds. There were hundreds, the largest I've ever seen, and I was so distracted by their beauty that I didn't notice nightfall. Then I heard a loud, hissing sound; all around, serpents slithered. I ran to a cave, blocking its entrance with a boulder. Serpents hissed outside all night. In the morning, they disappeared to hide from the bird, and I cautiously emerged.

I was examining the diamonds, no serpents in sight, when a curious thing happened: chunks of meat began falling from the sky. I suddenly remembered a story I'd heard about merchants who used meat to attract the giant bird. When it takes the meat, it also picks up the diamonds and brings them to its nest. There the merchants wait. They scare away the bird, taking the diamonds.

Again, I saw an opportunity for escape. I stuffed my pack with diamonds and tied myself to a piece of meat. Soon, the giant bird picked me up and took me on another thrilling ride to its nest. The merchants were astonished to see me there, but then they accused me of stealing their diamonds!

"Not so fast," I said, "I've gathered more diamonds than you ever could, and I have more than any of us will ever need. I'll share them in exchange for my rescue."

After that, we all sailed together, gathering riches. During the long days of our journey home, I told myself that this time I should stay. But every night, I dreamed of flying.

Answer the following questions.

1 Why does the author **most likely** include the detail about Sinbad stuffing his pack with diamonds?

- **A.** to show that Sinbad is clever, thinking ahead to his encounter with the merchants

- **B.** to show that Sinbad is greedy, wanting to keep all of the diamonds for himself

- **C.** to show that Sinbad is creative, using diamonds to get the bird to come to him

- **D.** to show that Sinbad is anxious, worried that someone else will take all the diamonds

> **Hint** Reread the part of the passage where Sinbad stuffs his pack with diamonds. How does he later use the diamonds?

2 The following question has two parts. First, answer Part A. Then, answer Part B.

Part A

Circle the words that describe Sinbad's character. Circle **all** that apply.

A. lazy

B. adventurous

C. timid

D. fearful

E. creative

F. determined

Part B

Find **two** sentences from the passage to support your response to Part A, and explain how these sentences support your choices.

_____

_____

_____

_____

_____

_____

Hint At the beginning of the passage, what does Sinbad plan to do? What does he do instead? What does he do to get off the islands? Sinbad's actions are clues to his character traits.

3 The following question has two parts. First, answer Part A. Then, answer Part B.

Part A

Circle the sentence that is a true statement about Sinbad.

Sinbad enjoys being on the islands so much that he wants to stay forever.
Sinbad wants to get off the islands, but he enjoys the adventure.
Sinbad does not enjoy anything about being on the islands and wants to get home immediately.

Part B

Underline **two** sentences in the passage that support this statement.

Hint Reread the parts of the passage that describe what Sinbad does while on the islands or what he says about the islands. How does he let you know whether he is enjoying himself?

4 A student wrote a response to the passage from "The Second Voyage of Sinbad the Sailor." Read the following sentences from her response.

Sinbad had a hard time escaping the two islands. The writer included details about his difficulties to show readers why Sinbad will never again go on an adventure.

Based on your reading of the story, do you agree with the student's opinion? Use text evidence to support your response. Write your response on the lines below.

_____

_____

_____

_____

_____

_____

_____

> **Hint** Look back to the part of the passage where Sinbad talks about being home. How can you use these details to support your response?

Use the Reading Guide to help you understand the passage.

Odysseus and the Cyclops

adapted from The Odyssey
by Homer

Reading Guide

What do you think Odysseus means when he says "life had other plans for my army and me"?

What do Odysseus's men want to do with the animals?

What do you learn about Odysseus's character when he insists that his men ask the cave owner for permission to take some food?

After we defeated the city of Troy, I thought our adventures were over. But life had other plans for my army and me. We had sailed for days, and decided to rest on an island. We tied our ship well and went off in search of food. Fruits and vegetables were scarce on the island, so we ventured farther into the forest, finally stumbling upon a cave. We found it filled with goats and sheep. Cheese and milk were stored against the cool cave walls.

It was clear that these animals had not arrived by accident. This cave had an owner, someone who raised sheep and goats.

My hungry army cried, "Let's take the animals and sail away now."

"No," I insisted, "We must ask the cave's owner for permission."

But I allowed that since we were starving, we could eat some of the cheese. I was sure that once we explained ourselves, whoever owned the cave would understand. I could never have imagined what would happen next.

We heard the cave's owner before we saw him. Each of his steps was like an earthquake. Before us was a Cyclops, a huge one-eyed monster named Polyphemus. He was holding a pile of tree trunks as if they were small sticks.

"Who dares enter my cave?" he roared. He picked up two of my men as if they were bugs, and dashed them to the floor. Rage burned in his giant eye as he lit a fire and threw the men upon it for his dinner. Before the rest of us could run, he blocked the cave's entrance with a large rock.

Reading Guide

What happens because of Odysseus's decision not to leave the cave before the owner arrives?

Notice how the author does not reveal all of Odysseus's plan at once. How does this encourage readers to read on?

What does Odysseus say when Polyphemus asks his name?

Even after Polyphemus went to sleep, there was nothing we could do. The rock was too big for us to move. We needed Polyphemus to do it. The next morning, he left the cave with two more men, locking us in again. If I didn't come up with a plan, we would all become dinner.

My men cried, "When he comes back, we'll attack him with our knives and swords!"

"No," I said, "Our tiny weapons would hurt him no more than a bee's sting."

I searched my mind, unsure of a solution, when I suddenly thought of the tree trunks Polyphemus had brought to the cave. I ordered my men to use their weapons to sharpen a tree trunk to a point. We hid the trunk in the back of the cave.

Now we needed a way to distract Polyphemus. I had in my pack a flower known to make people sleep. I heated some milk over the fire, and sprinkled the flowers in with some honey. When Polyphemus returned, I offered it to him.

"Before you enjoy another meaty dinner," I said, pretending to joke, "Please accept this sweet drink."

Polyphemus snatched the bowl and drank hungrily. "Tell me the name of the man who offers me this sweet, delicious nectar."

"My name is Noman," I said.

"Give me another bowl, Noman," Polyphemus roared. "Then it's time for the main course."

But before long, Polyphemus began to yawn. His giant eyelid drooped, and he fell asleep. Quickly, my men and I grabbed the tree trunk and thrust it into the fire until it was red hot. Then we drove it through the eye of Polyphemus, who woke bellowing with pain. Blinded, he swung his arms as my men and I hid in the corners of the cave. Then he called to the other Cyclops who lived outside the cave.

"Noman is hurting me!" he shrieked, "Noman is in my cave!"

The other Cyclops ignored him, saying, "If no man is hurting you, then nothing is wrong."

They moved on, leaving Polyphemus to roll away the rock blocking the cave. Seeing a way out, some of my men began to run.

"Stop," I hissed, "This is surely a trap. Polyphemus knows we'll run. He's waiting for us."

Instead, I looked to the wooly sheep in the cave. I showed my men how to roll underneath them and hold tight to the wool of their bellies. Unable to see, Polyphemus patted the backs of the sheep as they left one by one, but he did not know that we hung underneath.

We hiked silently to the shore and untied our ship. Only when we had set sail did I cry, "My name is not Noman. My name is Odysseus. Odysseus has outsmarted you!"

Enraged, Polyphemus called upon his father, Poseidon, god of the sea. He begged his father to punish us for blinding and taunting him.

To our misfortune, Poseidon sent great storms to disrupt our voyage. And so, even though we escaped, we could not go home as we planned. Instead, I spent ten long years at sea, thankful for my life, but sorry for my pride.

Answer the following questions.

1 Which sentences from the passage show that Odysseus is thinking ahead? Circle **all** that apply.

A. "We must ask the cave's owner for permission."

B. "Our tiny weapons would hurt him no more than a bee's sting."

C. "My name is Noman," I said.

D. "Stop," I hissed, "This is surely a trap."

E. "My name is Odysseus. Odysseus has outsmarted you!"

2 The following question has two parts. First, answer Part A. Then, answer Part B.

Part A

Underline the claim that is supported by the passage.

Claims	Odysseus is a brave leader who always thinks before he acts.
	Odysseus makes some decisions that end up hurting his men.
	Odysseus does not regret any of his actions.

Part B

What evidence from the story supports your response to part A? Write the evidence on the lines below.

_____

_____

_____

_____

3 Read the following excerpt from "Odysseus and the Cyclops." Underline **two** sentences that show how Odysseus is clever.

Seeing a way out, some of my men began to run.

"Stop," I hissed, "This is surely a trap. Polyphemus knows we'll run. He's waiting for us."

Instead, I looked to the wooly sheep in the cave. I showed my men how to roll underneath them and hold tight to the wool of their bellies.

4 Write each effect in the box next to its cause in the cause-and-effect chart.

| The other Cyclops don't help Polyphemus because they think nothing is wrong. |
| Poseidon sends storms to keep Odysseus and his men at sea. |
| Odysseus and his men escape the cave. |

Cause	Effect
Odysseus tells Polyphemus his name is Noman.	
Odysseus and his men hold on to sheep after Polyphemus is blinded.	
Odysseus taunts Polyphemus.	

5 Odysseus uses trickery to escape Polyphemus. Support this statement with **two** details from the passage.

Write your answer on the lines below.

_____

_____

_____

_____

_____

_____

6 Use what you have learned from reading "The Second Voyage of Sinbad the Sailor" and "Odysseus and the Cyclops" to write an essay analyzing how Sinbad and Odysseus were able to escape the situations they were in.
Be sure to:

- Explain each character's situation and how each escaped

- Describe each character's traits, comparing and contrasting Sinbad and Odysseus

- Explain how each character's thoughts, words, and actions help you understand his motivations

- Include details from each story to support your ideas

Plan your essay in the space below. Write your essay on the following pages.

Plan

Write your essay on the lines below.

Write a Narrative

Duplication any part of this book is prohibited by law. © 2015 Triumph Learning LLC

1 GETTING THE IDEA

Narrative writing tells a story to entertain the reader. Some narratives are fictional, while others tell true stories, but all narratives have characters, a setting, a plot, and a point of view.

- Choose a **setting's** time and location based on the kind of story you're telling. A fantasy story might take place in an imaginary world. A nonfiction narrative would take place where the events really happened.

- The **characters** perform the action in your narrative. Think about what you want them to be like and how they will show these traits through their words and actions.

- To plan the **plot**, decide on the **conflict**, or problem, the characters face. The events in your story will then move the characters toward a resolution of this conflict.

- **Point of view** refers to who is telling the story. The point of view affects how readers experience the story. A first-person point of view will help the reader experience the events as the narrator experiences them. If a third-person narrator tells the story, the reader may know things the characters don't.

Planning Your Narrative
To plan the plot, it can help to make an outline of what will happen in the beginning, middle, and end. The beginning of the story is where you introduce the conflict. That way, the characters can use the events of the story to work through it. The conclusion of your story, at the end, will show how the conflict is resolved.

The sample story outline below shows one way to plan a narrative.

Beginning	Middle	End
Conflict Ellie wants to learn how to play the keyboard, but Mom says the family can't afford a keyboard.	**Events** • Ellie talks to her music teacher about using a piano program in the school computer lab. • Ellie stays after school at the computer lab and uses the piano program to learn how to play the keyboard.	**Resolution** She shows Mom what she's learned, and the music teacher helps them work out a deal to borrow a keyboard from the school.

Writing Your Narrative Draft

Your goal when writing your narrative is to attract your readers at the beginning and keep them engaged until the end. Use the following techniques to make your writing clear and interesting.

When you **orient** your readers, you pull them into the story by introducing where it takes place and who the characters are. To get your readers' attention, you might start right in the middle of the action. Or you could start with an interesting description of the setting or characters. Whatever you decide, introduce the conflict early in the story. This will give your readers a reason to keep reading: to find out how the problem is solved.

A well-written narrative helps readers follow the **sequence** of events, so they know what happens first, next, and last.

- Pay attention to **pacing,** or how quickly the story moves. Long sentences full of description tend to move slowly, while short, action-packed sentences move quickly. As the writer, you can slow down or speed up the pacing to fit story events. For example, a description of the setting might move more slowly than a tense action scene.

- **Transitions** can help you move the story to suit your pacing needs. Words such as *then, soon, suddenly,* and *after that* show time passing and make the sequence of events clear.

When you write a description, use **sensory details** to tell how things look, feel, taste, smell, and sound. This helps bring your narrative, and your characters' experiences, to life. Use concrete and precise words to give readers a clear picture of what's going on.

Finally, let some details come out through the **dialogue**. Writing lively dialogue gives characters a unique voice and is a good way to show how characters respond to situations. Dialogue also helps readers get to know the characters better.

Revising and Editing Your Narrative

When you revise, put yourself in the reader's shoes. Ask yourself:

- ☐ Do I establish a situation with a setting, characters, and a plot conflict?

- ☐ Is the sequence of events clear and well-paced?

- ☐ Do I introduce and develop characters in an interesting way?

- ☐ Is there a consistent point of view?

- ☐ Do I use engaging dialogue and descriptive details?

- ☐ Does my ending follow from the events and make sense as a resolution?

- ☐ Is my narrative free of grammatical and spelling mistakes?

Language Spotlight • Commas

Use **commas** after the words *yes* and *no* and other words or phrases that introduce a sentence. Also, use commas to set off a question from the rest of the sentence. When you write dialogue, use a comma to separate the speaker's words from the rest of the sentence.

Yes, I do want to learn how to play the keyboard.

We can't afford a keyboard, can we?

"I can use this keyboard," Ellie said.

Read the following sentence. Where should you add commas?

"Yes you can borrow a keyboard from school" Ellie's teacher said.

Read the passage.

Hannah's Hiccups

"Could you hold this twig right here for me?" Amir asked his classmate Hannah as he reached for the glue. The two students were making a replica of a traditional Native American longhouse using natural materials they had collected at the park. Their paper bag full of small twigs and leaves was on the table next to a couple of bottles of glue and a picture of a longhouse from the Internet.

"HUH-UPP!" Hannah hiccupped loudly. The sudden, violent hiccup made her hand jerk. The twig she was holding knocked into the one next to it, causing their work-in-progress longhouse to collapse.

"Oh, no!" Hannah looked sadly at the ruined longhouse. "I guess we can—HUH-UPP!—start over."

"Not until you get rid of those hiccups," Amir said. "Try drinking some water. That should cure your hiccups." Hannah walked to the water fountain and took a few gulps.

"Did that work?" Amir asked when Hannah returned.

"HUH-UPP!" Hannah hiccupped again.

"I guess not," Amir said. "I know, try holding your breath."

Hannah inhaled until her lungs felt like they would burst; then she pressed her lips tightly together and pinched her nose with her thumb and index finger. After thirty seconds, she looked at Amir hopefully.

"Longer!" Amir encouraged.

Hannah held on for almost a minute, until, finally, she had to stop and gasp for air. Neither of them said a word as they waited to see if Amir's remedy worked.

"HUH-UPP!" Hannah slumped in her chair and Amir looked frustrated.

Suddenly, Amir shouted, "BOO!" right in Hannah's face.

Hannah jumped back. "You scared me!"

"That was the idea," Amir said. "I was trying to scare your hiccups away."

"I think it worked!" Hannah said happily, but then she hiccupped again.

As Hannah recovered from her last hiccup, Amir picked up the brown paper bag and dumped its contents onto the table. He handed the now empty bag to Hannah and said, "Hold this bag over your mouth while you breathe in and out."

Hannah did as instructed, and the paper bag inflated and deflated with each breath. It seemed to work at first, but then the muffled sound of a hiccup echoed through the bag.

Amir immediately had another idea for a cure. "Stick out your tongue as far as it will go, then pull on it with your right hand." When that didn't work, he had another suggestion, "Spin around clockwise and rub your stomach counterclockwise at the same time."

Hannah kept hiccupping while she twirled around and around, but soon she was too dizzy to continue. "I'm going to have the hiccups for the rest of my life," she despaired.

But Amir wasn't ready to give up. "It's time to try something new! Stick your fingers in your ears and burp the alphabet backward," Amir instructed.

"That's ridiculous!" Hannah shook her head.

"Just try it!" Amir insisted. "Or we'll never finish our social studies project."

Answer the following questions.

1 Read this excerpt from the passage.

> **Hannah did as instructed, and the paper bag inflated and deflated with each breath. It seemed to work at first, but then the muffled sound of a hiccup echoed through the bag.**

What details does the author use to help the reader visualize the scene?

_____

_____

_____

_____

Hint Which words help you see what's happening? Which words help you hear what's happening?

2 How does the author establish the situation in the passage?

A. The author begins with an interesting description of the setting.

B. The author begins in the middle of the action.

C. The author begins by telling the resolution.

D. The author begins by describing the characters.

Hint Think about what you learn first in the passage. How does the author introduce the conflict?

3 Read the following excerpt from the passage.

> Hannah kept hiccupping while she twirled around and around, but soon she was too dizzy to continue. "I'm going to have the hiccups for the rest of my life," she despaired.
>
> But Amir wasn't ready to give up. "It's time to try something new! Stick your fingers in your ears and burp the alphabet backward," Amir instructed.

Underline the sentence the author uses as a transition.

Hint A transition can be a word, phrase, or sentence that connects ideas in a text.

4 "Hannah's Hiccups" needs an ending. Write two paragraphs to finish the story. Use narrative strategies such as dialogue, description, and pacing, and show how the characters' problem is resolved.

_____

_____

_____

_____

_____

_____

_____

_____

_____

_____

_____

_____

_____

_____

_____

Use the Reading Guide to help you understand the passage.

The Red Oak Inn

Reading Guide

How does the author establish the conflict?

From what point of view is the story told?

What words does the author use to show the children's disappointment?

"This is lovely!" Grandma Edna gushed as she took in the cheerful suite of rooms she had booked for herself and her two grandchildren.

"It's nice," ten-year-old Debbie replied, forcing a smile. Staying at a boring old inn was not her idea of a vacation.

"So what is there to do here?" Jesse, Debbie's older brother, wanted to know. He suspected that he already knew the answer—nothing!

Edna appeared not to notice her grandchildren's lack of enthusiasm. "The Red Oak Inn has an exceptionally fine library of great historical significance," she answered. "I can't wait to see it!"

Jesse and Debbie looked at each other in disbelief. Wasting their vacation looking at dusty books and faded photographs was even worse than they imagined.

Staying at the Red Oak Inn in the Ohio River Valley was all Grandma Edna's idea. Grandma Edna had traced her family tree back to African American slaves who had traveled along the Underground Railroad, a trail of safe houses where slaves could rest and hide as they made their way north to freedom. Grandma Edna suspected that her ancestors had come through this part of Ohio. She was compiling a list of places where they had stayed on the dangerous route to freedom. She wanted to chronicle their journey for her grandchildren and future descendants, so they could better appreciate their own proud heritage.

How does the dialogue reveal how the characters feel?

What transition words and phrases does the author use to help you follow the sequence of events?

Think about the way the author describes the inn. What words help you picture the inn in your mind?

Debbie and Jesse had made it very clear that they would prefer to go to a water park. They had learned about the Underground Railroad at school. It was ancient history to them. They did not identify with their slave ancestors the way their grandma did. By the time Jesse and Debbie were born, the United States was a different place than it had been in the 1960s when Grandma Edna was a child living in a segregated Southern town.

"At least the food is good," Jesse whispered to Debbie as the waiter cleared their plates. Before dinner, Jesse and Debbie had explored the Red Oak Inn. The old mansion hadn't looked so sizable from the outside, yet they quickly got lost among the labyrinth of corridors and staircases hiding behind unmarked doors. It was only when they heard Grandma Edna calling their names that they were able to follow her voice back to their suite to dress for dinner.

Grandma Edna thanked the waiter, daintily dabbed her mouth with a linen napkin, and stood up from the table. "That was delicious," she said. "Now, let's go to the library!" Debbie and Jesse followed her, unenthusiastically, to a large room with floor-to-ceiling shelves packed with books of every shape and size.

Debbie recognized some of the titles. She pulled a classic mystery from one of the shelves and sat down to read. Jesse plopped down in an armchair and sulked. There wasn't a television anywhere at this inn, and no Internet either. He watched as his grandma pulled book after book from the shelf marked "Ross County History." Then Grandma Edna pulled out a small notebook and pencil from her handbag and began scribbling away.

Reading Guide

How does the author show that Grandma Edna and the children have spent a long time in the library?

Compare Debbie and Jesse's attitude at the beginning of the story to their attitude at the end. How does the author show the changes in their attitudes?

Why does Jesse's mood change from boredom to excitement?

Jesse must have dozed off, because the next thing he knew his sister was shaking him awake.

"You've got to take a look at this!" She was holding what looked like an old sketchbook, open to a page with a drawing of a big, beautiful mansion. "I think this has something to do with the Underground Railroad," she said.

Jesse rubbed the sleep from his eyes. "It looks like this place, only not so old and grubby."

Together, Jesse and Debbie flipped through the pages of the book. There were other drawings in the book of staircases and furnished rooms. Some of them looked familiar.

"I know where that is!" Jesse jumped up from the chair. A moment ago he had fallen asleep from boredom. Now he felt his body vibrating with energy. "Follow me!"

Jesse raced to one of the back staircases they had seen earlier when they had gotten lost.

"Those pictures in the book are like directions," Jesse said.

"But directions to where?" Debbie asked. She still had the book in her hands.

"That's what we're going to find out!" Jesse said confidently.

Answer the following questions.

1 Which of these sentences from the passage use transitions? Choose **all** that apply.

A. Then Grandma Edna pulled out a small notebook and pencil from her handbag and began scribbling away.

B. Jesse rubbed the sleep from his eyes.

C. Together, Jesse and Debbie flipped through the pages of the book.

D. A moment ago he had fallen asleep from boredom.

E. Now he felt his body vibrating with energy.

2 The following events are from the passage. In each box, write the number 2, 3, 4, or 5 so that the events are in the correct order.

| 1 | Jesse, Debbie, and Grandma Edna arrive at the Red Oak Inn. |

| | Jesse, Debbie, and Grandma Edna eat dinner at the inn. |

| | Jesse dozes off. |

| | Debbie and Jesse get lost at the inn. |

| | Debbie, Jessie, and Grandma Edna go to the library. |

| 6 | Jesse recognizes pictures in an old book about the inn and leads Debbie to a back staircase at the inn. |

3 Read the following excerpt from the passage.

> **Debbie recognized some of the titles. She pulled a classic mystery from one of the shelves and sat down to read. Jesse plopped down in an armchair and sulked. There wasn't a television anywhere at this inn, and no Internet either.**

Rewrite this excerpt using dialogue.

_____

_____

_____

_____

_____

_____

_____

_____

4 Underline **two** sentences in the passage that show how the author describes the different backgrounds of Grandma Edna and her grandchildren.

5 The following question has two parts. First, answer part A. Then, answer part B.

Part A

Which of these sentences **best** describes Debbie's feelings about staying at the inn at the beginning of the passage?

A. She is excited to stay at the inn and learn about the Underground Railroad.

B. She isn't excited about staying at the inn, but she doesn't want to hurt her grandmother's feelings.

C. She is annoyed that she has to stay at the inn and wants to make that clear to her grandmother.

D. She is less enthusiastic than her brother about staying at the inn.

Part B

Which excerpt from the passage **best** supports the idea that Debbie's feelings about the inn change over the course of the story?

A. "It's nice," ten-year-old Debbie replied, forcing a smile.

B. Jesse and Debbie looked at each other in disbelief.

C. Debbie recognized some of the titles. She pulled a classic mystery from one of the shelves and sat down to read.

D. "You've got to take a look at this!" She was holding what looked like an old sketchbook, open to a page with a drawing of a big, beautiful mansion.

6 Use what you have learned about the characters and setting of "The Red Oak Inn" to write what happens next. Remember that your writing should include narrative techniques such as description, dialogue, and pacing, and should build on the events that already happened in the story.

Plan your narrative in the space below. Write your narrative on the following pages.

<table>
<tr><td> Plan

</td></tr>
</table>

Write your narrative on the lines below.

W.5.7, W.5.8, W.5.9.b, L.5.2.d

Research Skills

Writing often requires **research**, the process of finding facts and information in various sources. The research process usually includes the following steps: identifying and narrowing down a research question; performing searches related to your question; choosing the right print and digital sources; and taking careful notes on those sources.

Selecting a Research Question

A **research question** is a question you form about a topic that will guide your research and, eventually, your writing. First, brainstorm topics that interest you or that relate to the writing prompt you have been given. Eliminate ideas that are too broad or too limited for your assignment.

Next, come up with questions that identify what you want to find out through your research. Choose the strongest question as your research question. A good research question could be, "Why are solar panels better for the environment than other energy sources?"

Performing Searches

The **library** offers a wealth of information in the form of books, magazines, journals, newspapers, encyclopedias, almanacs, and many other print and media formats. It is an ideal place to start your research.

The **Internet** is an ever-growing collection of information. When performing Web searches, select information carefully. Not all information online is accurate and reliable. Education and government Web sites are good sources of reliable information. Avoid sites created by individuals who are not experts in the subject area.

Choosing Appropriate Sources

Any source you use should be accurate, relevant, and credible. **Accurate** sources provide correct information. **Relevant** sources relate to the topic you are researching. **Credible** sources are trustworthy and believable.

Let's say that you are researching gardening. Discuss with a partner whether the following sources are accurate, relevant, and/or credible.

- an online blog by an expert gardener

- a private journal of a gardener

- an encyclopedia entry about gardening

Remember that sources with strong opinions that focus on feelings are generally less reliable than fact-based sources.

Taking Notes

When taking notes, gather only information that relates to your topic. Choose textual evidence that directly supports your ideas and conclusions. Any other information is unnecessary.

Suppose you want to research the best conditions for growing squash. Which piece of information is *not* relevant to your topic?

- Squash can be cooked in different ways.

- Squash grow best in full sunlight.

- Moist soil should be used when planting squash.

It is important that you do not **plagiarize**, or pass off someone else's work as your own. You can avoid plagiarism by quoting, paraphrasing, or summarizing the source and attributing, or naming, the source. On the next page, read the passage from a source. Then, look at the different ways the information can be represented in a research paper.

Teri Talks Squash

Summer squash is very different from winter squash. Winter squash has a tough skin that is inedible. Summer squash has skin that is more tender and tasty.

Quote: Put the original text in quotation marks with a reference to the author or source.	In *Teri Talks Squash*, Teri explains, "Summer squash is very different from winter squash."
Paraphrase: Retell the source material in your own words with a reference to the author or source.	*Teri Talks Squash* explains that the skins of summer and winter squash are different. Winter squash is tough and cannot be eaten. Summer squash is softer and edible.
Summarize: Explain the overall ideas you have learned from the source.	Winter squash has tough skin that cannot be eaten. Summer squash has tender skin that can be eaten.

Finally, use a **bibliography** or **works cited** page to list information about all of the sources you used. For each entry, include the source's title, author's name, and date of publication. There are many different styles for showing this information, so check with your teacher to see which style you should follow.

Language Spotlight • Indicate Titles of Works

These guidelines explain how to show titles of different works.

Work	Style	Examples
book, play, movie, magazine, journal, Web site, newspaper	italics or underlining	*Hatchet*, *The Sound of Music*, *The New York Times*, www. nasa.gov
short story, article, poem, song, chapter, essay	quotation marks	"What is Pink?" "Over the Rainbow" "The Road Not Taken"

Now write your own examples for each types of work.

Read the passage.

Driverless Cars: The Future Is Now

Picture yourself behind the wheel of a car driving down the street. You turn and slow down as you carefully park between two parked cars. It is a typical event when driving—only this time you aren't driving at all. Instead, you are talking on the phone, reading a book, or even watching a movie as the car carries you to your destination and parks itself.

Sound like the stuff of science fiction? If you said *yes*, you wouldn't be the first to doubt the reality of driverless cars. These vehicles, though, are very real. They exist right here and now.

Driverless cars are exactly what they sound like—cars without drivers. They drive themselves. A person may sit behind the wheel and tell the car where to go, but the car is programmed to travel to a location without driving help from a person. Essentially, everyone in a driverless car is a passenger who can simply enjoy the ride.

While these cars are undoubtedly fun to experience, they are being developed primarily to make roads safer. In fact, some manufacturers estimate a 90 percent decrease in injuries from accidents with the use of driverless cars. These estimates are based on the sophisticated technology used by the cars. Some of the features are already familiar to many drivers.

Automatic features like anti-lock brakes and cruise control have been in cars for decades and make some operations driver-independent. Self-parking cars debuted in the mid-2000s. Completely driverless cars, however, take those semi-driverless cars to the next level. In them, cruise control becomes adaptive and can react to the environment. Using something called a "pre-safe system," the car's cameras and sensors identify hazards. Then the sensors "tell" the car to slow down or turn to help avoid accidents.

Free Ranging On Grid (FROG) is a technology used to get from one point to another. In its most basic form, this technology consists of a computer with a map. It calculates a route from point A to point B.

As the car moves through traffic, its navigating computer and sensors are always aware of dangers on the road. They do not get distracted and therefore respond to every unexpected change or threat that suddenly appears on the road. They also do not get tired, so driver fatigue is not a danger while driving, either. In general, these factors help make driverless driving safer than manned driving!

So far, the response to driverless cars has been mixed. Some states have shied away from giving complete control to a car. Other states, such as California, Florida, and Nevada, have welcomed the idea. They have already passed laws that allow driverless cars to be tested on public roads. More states are expected to follow in the years to come. Research suggests that a working model might be available for the public to buy as early as 2017. Manufacturers will have to work on lowering the price tag, though. Currently, the technology costs about $150,000 per car! Still, in just a few years drivers may be settling in behind the wheel of their trusty vehicles, leaving the actual driving to their cars.

Answer the following questions.

1 Summarize the main points of the passage. What are the most important ideas?

_____

_____

_____

_____

_____

> **Hint** Remember that the most important ideas are often given in the first sentence of a paragraph. Review the first sentence of each paragraph to identify these main ideas and use them to summarize the passage.

2 The following question has two parts. First, answer Part A. Then, answer Part B.

Part A

For class, Kamil will write a report describing how driverless cars work. Read the following paragraph from "Driverless Cars: The Future Is Now."

> **Picture yourself behind the wheel of a car driving down the street. You turn and slow down as you carefully park between two parked cars. It is a typical event when driving—only this time you aren't driving at all. Instead, you are talking on the phone, reading a book, or even watching a movie as the car carries you to your destination.**

Underline the details in the paragraph that give information about how driverless cars work.

Part B

Paraphrase the details you underlined in Part A to show how Kamil could include the information in his report.

_____

_____

_____

_____

_____

_____

Hint Underline the part of the paragraph that describes how a driverless car is different from a regular car. Describe the experience in your own words.

3 Read the following paragraph from a student's research report.

> **Driverless cars can provide many benefits for individuals and society. Safety, accident, and traffic conditions would all show great improvement if this new technology were utilized. Although there are certainly some related challenges to overcome, the benefits more than outweigh the problems.**

What evidence from "Driverless Cars: The Future Is Now" can the student use to support the opinion presented in the paragraph? Choose **all** that apply.

A. Driverless cars are exactly what they sound like—cars without drivers.

B. Sensors do not get distracted and therefore respond to every unexpected change or threat that suddenly appears on the road.

C. Sensors do not get tired, so driver fatigue is not a danger while driving either.

D. Some states have shied away from giving complete control of driving to a car.

E. Research suggests that a working model might be available for the public to buy as early as 2017.

F. Currently the technology costs about $150,000 per car!

Hint First, determine the student's position on driverless cars. Then, look for evidence that relates to this position.

4 Read the following excerpt from a source on driverless cars.

> **A new race has begun in the automotive industry. It is a race to create new and improved driverless cars. Automakers realize that the public is interested in this idea, and they want to get in on the action. One way they are doing this is by adding cameras and sensors to aid drivers in existing car models. Cameras and sensors give driverless cars more information to navigate and react to changes around them.**

Which sentence from the excerpt adds new information about the topic that is **not** included in "Driverless Cars: The Future Is Now"?

_____

_____

Hint What is the topic of the passage? Look for a sentence in the excerpt that provides related information.

Use the Reading Guide to help you understand the passage.

The Pros and Cons of Driverless Cars

Reading Guide

How is the passage organized?

What details support the opinion that driverless cars are a good idea?

Does the author do a good job of presenting the argument for driverless cars?

Every day we come face to face with new and improved technology. The latest innovation in the automotive industry is the driverless car—a vehicle that drives itself. It does not need a human driver. While this is definitely an exciting idea, is it a *good* one? Opinions vary on the topic, with valid points for each side.

Full Speed Ahead

Whoever thought of driverless cars is a genius! The benefits of this technology are too numerous to count. The most obvious one is that it makes riding in a car much more productive. People live busy lives. They are always multi-tasking. When they drive, though, they must focus on the road. With a driverless car, passengers can safely do business on the phone, read, or work on the computer. The idea is simple but revolutionary!

Driverless cars are helpful for seniors and people with disabilities. Some are unable to drive a car, and they lose a sense of independence as a result. They must rely on others to drive them to where they need to go. Driverless cars eliminate that problem and help people regain freedoms they lost.

In addition, the ride is much safer than when people are driving. This is because the cars can react faster and "see" all around them. Car manufacturers have predicted that using driverless cars will lead to fewer traffic accidents, traffic jams, and costs associated with accidents.

Compare the two viewpoints. Think about the different points each author makes.

How does the author of "Hit the Brakes" discuss safety in a different way from how the author of "Full Speed Ahead" discusses safety?

There could be environmental benefits of driverless cars too. Cars today are built heavy in order to withstand crashes. If driverless cars really made driving safer, then cars could be built lighter. Lighter cars demand less fuel and produce less pollution. Also, people might be more likely to share driverless cars rather than feel that they have to have their own. This cooperation could reduce the resources needed to build cars and the pollution created by having so many cars on the road. With fewer cars, there would be less traffic, fewer traffic jams, and even less pollution as cars get off the road faster.

As you can see, there are many benefits to having driverless cars—far too many to let this opportunity pass us by!

Jamie Singh
St. Louis, Missouri

Hit the Brakes

Some say that driverless cars are the way to go, but I say STOP! Adding computerized cars to our already-crowded roads is the worst thing we could possibly do. Do you really want to put your life in the hands of a car? Driverless cars are supposed to make you safe, but what if they break down? What if they do not sense a hazard in their path? The consequences could be terrible.

Beyond these safety concerns, there are other problems related to putting driverless cars on the road. Many state and federal driving laws would have to be reviewed and rewritten. Who is responsible for a speeding ticket or even an accident when a driverless car is involved—is it the owner of the car or the car maker? Do you even need a driver's license to own and operate a driverless car? How old do you have to be to "drive" one? Currently, some states are revising their own laws, but with not every state doing this, what happens if you take a driverless car across a state border? Legislation would need a major overhaul!

Reading Guide

Which details would be useful when writing a report about driverless cars?

Which details would not be useful? What makes them less useful?

There are concerns about the economic impact. Many people depend on cars for their livelihood. Drivers of buses, delivery vehicles, taxis, and limos could be forced out of work and might have a very difficult time finding new jobs in a different field.

The cost of a driverless car is very high—well over $100,000. Few people could afford it. It is not clear how the research for all of the new parts and special roads will be financed. Even though private companies want to develop the cars for their own profit, will taxpayers have to pay for the public roads or tracks that these new cars will run on?

Driverless cars may seem like a good idea at first, but they have many risks and problems.

Carolyn Leonard
Decatur, Georgia

Two Sides, One Future

The idea of driverless cars is certainly a hot topic. It will continue to be debated as manufacturers move closer and closer to a finished product. Ultimately, the issues that surround driverless cars about responsibility and costs will need to be resolved. Questions about who will bear the costs and how the downsides will be managed must be weighed against the potential benefits, such as the promise of a safer, more enjoyable ride. Given the different sides of the issue, what do you think about driverless cars?

Answer the following questions.

1 This question has two parts. First, answer Part A. Then, answer Part B.

Part A

A student is writing a research paper about legislation related to driverless cars. Which conclusion can the student make based on the evidence provided in "The Pros and Cons of Driverless Cars"?

A. States will not have a difficult time agreeing on common laws.

B. There is much confusion and uncertainty surrounding the laws.

C. All states generally have the same set of rules and regulations.

D. Federal laws will inform the states about which rules to follow.

Part B

Which sentence from the passage **best** supports the answer to Part A?

A. Beyond these safety concerns, there are other problems related to putting driverless cars on the road.

B. In addition, the ride is much safer than when people are driving.

C. Currently, states are revising their own laws separately, but with not every state doing this, what happens if you take a driverless car across a state border?

D. The benefits of this technology are too numerous to count.

2 Read the following notes a student took based on the passage "The Pros and Cons of Driverless Cars." Use information from the passage to add one more detail to each column of the chart.

Pros of Driverless Cars	Cons of Driverless Cars
• They free up riders to be more productive. • They help seniors and people with disabilities regain their freedom. • They reduce the likelihood of accidents and improve safety. • _____	• It is not clear who is responsible for tickets and accidents. • State and federal laws would have to be revised. • Some people could lose their jobs. • _____

Answer the following questions about both passages in this lesson.

3 You are writing a report on how driverless cars improve safety on the road.

Read the following paragraphs.

While these cars are undoubtedly fun to experience, they are being developed primarily to make roads safer. In fact, some manufacturers estimate a 90% decrease in injuries from accidents with the use of driverless cars. These estimates are based on the sophisticated technology used by the cars. Some of the features are already familiar to many drivers.

In addition, the ride is much safer than when people are driving. This is because the cars can react faster and "see" all around them. Car manufacturers have predicted that using driverless cars will lead to fewer traffic accidents, traffic jams, and costs associated with accidents.

Underline **one** detail about safety from **each** passage that would be useful to include in your report.

4 Farah is writing a research report about driverless cars. She has gathered some information from "Driverless Cars: The Future Is Now" and "The Pros and Cons of Driverless Cars."

Read the following paragraphs from the passages.

"Driverless Cars: The Future Is Now"

As the car moves through traffic, its navigating computer and sensors are always aware of dangers on the road. They do not get distracted and therefore respond to every unexpected change or threat that suddenly appears on the road. They also do not get tired, so driver fatigue is not a danger while driving either. In general, these factors help to make driverless driving safer than manned driving!

"The Pros and Cons of Driverless Cars"

In addition, the ride is much safer than when people are driving. This is because the cars can react faster and "see" all around them. Car manufacturers have predicted that using driverless cars will lead to fewer traffic accidents, traffic jams, and costs associated with accidents.

On which point do the two sources agree? Choose **all** that apply.

A. Computers respond faster than people.

B. Driver fatigue is a major problem.

C. Driverless cars are safer than cars driven by people.

D. Some people should not be allowed to drive on the road.

E. Driverless cars will reduce traffic jams and pollution.

5 A student is creating a list of sources for a report about the computerized system in driverless cars. Read the following source titles and descriptions.

The Father of the Automobile: The Early Years
a biography of Henry Ford's childhood

A New Kind of Driver
an article about the first racecar drivers in America

What Makes a Car Driverless?
a Web site that discusses the parts of a driverless car and how they work

Hyperdrive
a science fiction story about gravity-free, driverless cars that race in space

Technical Auto
a science journal that explains the delicate processes involved in automobile sensors

Robotic Systems in New Cars
an article about how new cars are being equipped with devices that can read environments and predict accidents

Which are relevant and credible sources the student can use in his report? Circle them in the list above.

6 You have read two passages describing driverless cars. Both include facts and details about this technology. The two texts are:

- "Driverless Cars: The Future Is Now"

- "The Pros and Cons of Driverless Cars"

Consider the type of information each author provides to describe driverless cars.

Write an essay that summarizes the information in both texts. In your essay, indicate which text you believe provided more relevant and useful details about the topic. Remember to use textual evidence to support your ideas.

Plan your essay in the space below. Write your essay on the following pages.

Plan

Write your essay on the lines below.

W.5.2.a–e, L.5.1.d

Write an Informative or Explanatory Text

Informative or **explanatory text** provides information or explains something about a topic to readers. This type of text includes articles, essays, and reports with well-chosen facts and details.

State Your Topic

A **topic sentence** appears in the opening paragraph and explains the central idea of your text. It should be written clearly so the topic is obvious to readers. All other ideas in the text should relate to the topic sentence.

The following is an example of a well-written topic sentence.

> The use of solar energy to make electricity is slowly starting to rise across the United States.

Develop Your Topic

Develop your informative essay with well-chosen facts and examples. They should all be **relevant**, or related to the topic. When you use information from a source, you should state it in your own words. However, sometimes it is necessary to include an exact quote from a source. In that case, use quotation marks around the exact words from the source. You should also give the name of the source from which you took the quote.

Read the following facts. Which best relates to the topic described in the topic sentence above? Underline it.

- Germany produces more solar power than any other country in Europe.

- The sun is the source of not only solar power, but also wind power.

- About 10 percent of electricity in the United States could come from solar power by 2025.

Organize Your Ideas

Your article, essay, or report should include an introduction, body paragraphs, and a conclusion. You can use an outline or a graphic organizer, such as a chart, to organize your ideas.

Introduction	Body Paragraphs	Conclusion
• include the topic sentence • preview the ideas and facts that will be discussed	• present strong, relevant supporting facts and details • use a logical order	• sum up the information or explanation presented in the text • include a final thought for readers

Write Your Draft

Style When you write, use a style that fits your audience and purpose. For an informational or explanatory text, you should use a **formal style**. Your audience is likely your teacher and fellow students, so your writing should sound academic, not conversational. Avoid the use of contractions, slang, and shorthand.

Precise Language Your audience may not be familiar with your topic. Be sure to define any elaborate domain-specific words. Also use words that clearly explain the information you present. Exact nouns, verbs, adjectives, and adverbs will make your meaning clear and present your facts in a way your readers can understand.

Transitions Using transitions will help readers better understand how your ideas are connected. **Transitions** are words and phrases that show a change in thought between sentences and paragraphs. Use words such as *however*, *especially*, *in addition*, and *in contrast* to connect your ideas.

Provide a Conclusion

An informative or explanatory text should end with a **conclusion** that sums up the information in the text. It should leave readers with a final thought about the topic. For an informative paragraph or short essay, you need to include only a concluding statement. For a longer text, such as a report, include a concluding paragraph or section.

Review Your Work

After you have finished writing, reread your work to make sure it is clear and well organized. Use the following checklist to guide you as you make changes to your work.

- ☐ Is my topic sentence clear?

- ☐ Are the facts and details I included relevant to my topic?

- ☐ Do I use a formal style, precise language, and transitions?

- ☐ Does my conclusion sum up the topic for readers?

- ☐ Is my writing free of grammar and spelling errors?

Language Spotlight • Shifts in Verb Tense

A **verb** is a word that describes an action or a state of being. **Verb tense** explains when the action or state of being takes place.

- In the **past tense**, the action already happened: *I ate lunch earlier*.

- In the **present tense**, the action is happening now: *I am eating lunch now*.

- In the **future tense**, the action has not happened yet: *I will eat lunch later*.

Be sure to use the same verb tense throughout a sentence. Shifts in verb tense are incorrect and can confuse readers. Read the following sentence. The underlined words show a shift in verb tense. How should the sentence be revised?

Yesterday, we packed a lunch, <u>will walk</u> to the park, and <u>have</u> a picnic.

Read the passage.

Energy from the Earth

We rely on fossil fuels, such as oil and coal, to heat homes, create electricity, and cook food. However, these resources are nonrenewable. This means that one day they will run out. Therefore, many nations have begun to use renewable resources. Unlike fossil fuels, renewable resources will not run out. These resources rely on natural sources such as the sun, wind, or water, and are continually replenished. One resource, called geothermal energy, is found within the earth and can provide a great deal of power.

The word *geothermal* helps explain what this power is. The word comes from two Greek words: *geo*, which means "earth," and *therme*, which means "heat." So, geothermal energy is heat found within Earth.

There is a great deal of heat underneath our feet. Earth has a core four thousand miles below the surface. There, temperatures rise above 7,600°F (4,204°C). The core's outer layer is magma, or melted rock. It heats the water underground. This water can reach the surface as pools of hot water called springs. Sometimes, water bursts out in jets of hot steam called geysers. We can also dig wells to reach water heated by magma to use for energy.

There are two ways to use geothermal energy, for heat or electricity. Geothermal heat pumps send hot water into buildings to keep them warm. Geothermal power plants use hot water to run machines that generate electricity.

As of 2010, twenty-four nations had geothermal power plants. The United States creates more geothermal power than any other country. Most United States geothermal power plants are in Hawaii, California, and other western states.

There are several benefits to using geothermal power. For one thing, it's a renewable resource because Earth's core continuously creates heat. Using geothermal energy also is cleaner than burning coal or oil. As more and more nations use geothermal energy, it may answer our energy problems.

A geyser emits hot steam in Yellowstone National Park in Wyoming.

Answer the following questions.

1 These sentences could be included in the passage. Which one is the **best** example of formal style?

   A. It would be stupid not to use renewable sources of energy.

   B. I think tapping into geothermal energy is a really cool idea.

   C. The use of geothermal power has become common.

   D. It is super-hot at Earth's core, which is the center of the planet.

> **Hint** A formal style avoids the use of slang or other kinds of informal language.

2 Circle two examples of transition words or phrases in paragraph 1 of the passage.

> **Hint** Remember, writers include transition words or phrases to connect ideas in a text.

3 This question has two parts. First, answer Part A. Then, answer Part B.

Part A

Which is the topic sentence of the passage?

A. We rely on fossil fuels, such as oil and coal, to heat homes, create electricity, and cook food.

B. However, these resources are nonrenewable.

C. Therefore, many nations have begun to use renewable resources.

D. One resource, called geothermal energy, is found within the earth and can provide a great deal of power.

Part B

Explain why the answer to Part A is an example of a well-written topic sentence.

_____

_____

_____

> **Hint** This question asks you to do two things. For Part A, think about what the details in the passage are mostly about. For Part B, think about the purpose of a topic sentence and how it helps readers.

4 Explain how the author uses facts and details to help readers understand what geothermal energy is.

_____

_____

_____

_____

> **Hint** In your answer, describe the facts and details the writer includes that help explain what geothermal energy is and where it is found. Be sure to include all the relevant details from the passage in your response.

Use the Reading Guide to help you understand the passage.

Shipping Power under the Sea

Reading Guide

Look for any domain-specific words in the passage. Pay attention to how the author defines and explains the words. Identify context clues that can help you understand their meanings.

What transition words or phrases has the author included to connect ideas?

More and more nations are turning to geothermal power. About twenty-four countries produce electricity from geothermal energy. Iceland is a big producer of geothermal energy. In fact, the capital city of Iceland, Reykjavik (RAY-kyuh-vik), runs on geothermal power. It uses this form of energy to heat homes, offices, and even swimming pools. Soon, Iceland might provide energy not only to its people. It might also supply geothermal power to other nations.

Iceland makes a great deal of geothermal energy for two reasons. One, it has a number of hot springs and geysers. Two, there are several volcanoes in Iceland. A volcano is another source of geothermal heat. For these reasons, Iceland can produce a lot of geothermal power cheaply.

In fact, Iceland produces more geothermal power than its people can use. As a result, some people have started thinking about selling some of this power. The nation's main power company is working on a "submarine interconnector." That's a name for an underwater cable. This cable would act as a really big extension cord. It would stretch across the North Atlantic ocean. Through this method, Iceland could send power to parts of Europe.

A similar cable that runs from Norway to the Netherlands is currently the longest underwater cable in the world. The interconnector from Iceland would be three times as long, extending about seven hundred miles to northern Scotland. From there, it would stretch another twelve hundred miles to the rest of Europe.

Some people in Iceland think this plan is a great idea. Selling geothermal power would boost the country's economy. It would also encourage other countries to use clean energy. After all, geothermal power is much cleaner than fossil fuels.

Reading Guide

Does the author use formal or informal language? How do you know?

What different views about the interconnector does the author present? Underline words or phrases the author uses to connect comparisons and contrasts of the ideas.

What final thought does the writer leave for the reader?

However, other people worry about the cost of the project. It would take more than $2 billion to install the interconnector. Opponents of the plan wonder how the nation will raise this money. They also worry about taking energy away from Iceland. They want to make sure the country will have all the power it needs in a crisis or for future generations.

Still others are concerned about how the interconnector will affect the environment. To collect enough energy to send overseas, companies would need to build more power plants. That would involve a lot of construction in rural areas. Also, while geothermal power is cleaner than burning fossil fuels, it is not perfect. It creates waste water. It also releases a gas called hydrogen sulfide that smells like rotten eggs. So building more power plants might have some negative consequences.

A group called the Left-Green Movement would rather see any extra electricity go to greenhouses, fish farms, and other industries in Iceland. In 2013, the group's leader told the *New York Times*, "We need to create jobs, not rely on bulk exports."

For now, the people of Iceland are thinking about their options. People are thinking of all the reasons for and against the project. If anyone finds a plan most people agree with, the country will start to work on it. Maybe one day, geothermal energy from Iceland will power places as far away as London and Paris.

A geothermal power plant in Iceland

Answer the following questions.

1 How does the author develop the topic in the passage? Use details from the text to support your answer.

_____

_____

_____

_____

_____

2 Which detail is **most** relevant to the topic of the passage? Underline it.

Southern Europe has established a large solar power project.
The interconnector would be made of miles of copper cable.
A United States company has set up aluminum processing plants in Iceland.

3 Which of the following transition words or phrases does the author use in the passage? Choose **all** that apply.

A. Especially

B. As a result

C. In spite of

D. Therefore

E. Additionally

F. However

4 The following question has two parts. First, answer Part A. Then, answer Part B.

Part A

A student is writing about geothermal energy. Which of the following sentences has a shift in verb tense?

A. An interconnector that stretches from Norway to the Netherlands is currently the largest interconnector in the world.

B. The term geothermal energy makes people thought of Iceland.

C. Some people worry about the cost of the project and think the country does not have enough funds to complete it.

D. One day, Iceland may have the largest interconnector in the world and sell power to other parts of Europe.

Part B

Write the sentence you chose in Part A using the correct verb tense.

_____

_____

_____

5 Read the following excerpt from the passage.

In fact, the capital city of Iceland, Reykjavik, runs on geothermal power.

Which detail from the passage does the author use to help the reader understand the meaning of geothermal power?

A. About twenty-four countries produce electricity from geothermal energy.

B. Iceland makes a great deal of geothermal energy for two reasons.

C. As a result, some people in Iceland have started thinking about selling some of this power.

D. It would also encourage other countries to use clean energy.

E. It creates waste water.

6 Imagine you work for a geothermal power plant in Iceland. Your job is to write a report explaining why the country should build a "submarine interconnector" to Europe. Write an essay explaining the purpose of the interconnector. You should also provide readers with background information on geothermal energy and how it is used. Use information from "Energy from the Earth" and "Shipping Power under the Sea" to support your ideas.

Plan your explanatory essay in the space below. Write your explanatory essay on the following pages.

Plan

Write your explanatory essay on the lines below.

Write an Opinion

① GETTING THE IDEA

Is there an idea or a cause you feel strongly about? You can use your strong feelings to write an opinion piece. In an **opinion piece**, you offer the reader your **point of view**, or personal beliefs about a topic. Your point of view includes your opinion. An **opinion** is a statement that cannot be proved.

Introduce Your Position

The first step in writing an opinion piece is deciding on a topic. Then, think about your position or point of view. State your point of view clearly so the reader understands what it is. Read how one student introduced his topic and point of view in a letter to his school newspaper. What is his position?

> Our principals should reconsider their plan to eliminate fifth and sixth grade recess.

Support Your Position

You need to support your opinion with reasons, facts, and details. When your opinion is well supported, you have a better chance of getting your readers to agree with your point of view. Research your topic to find facts that show your point of view is a good one. Include those facts in your writing. For example, simply stating that recess is good for students is not as effective as providing evidence that supports the statement.

Read how the writer used facts to support his position on recess in his letter to the school newspaper.

> The plan to eliminate recess is a bad idea. According to a 2012 report by the American Academy of Pediatrics, children who have recess can concentrate better and stay on task during their afternoon schoolwork.

A strong opinion piece recognizes opposing points of view on the topic. In your writing, you should include points of view that oppose yours and respond to them by showing why your position is better.

Organize Your Ideas

Think about your reasons and supporting facts when organizing your ideas. List the strongest reasons first. Usually the strongest reasons are the ones you can back up with the most facts and details. Return to your sources as much as necessary for additional facts and details that would make your reasons stronger.

Use **transitions**, or words and phrases that show a change in thought, to ensure that each paragraph flows smoothly into the next. You can also use transitions to show how your reasons support your point of view. Examples of transitions include *while*, *for example*, and *therefore*.

Use a graphic organizer like the one below to plan and organize your ideas.

Point of View	Doing away with recess is a bad idea.
Reason 1	Student need the exercise they get at recess.
Supporting facts	• helps student at risk for obesity
	• makes student more active before and after school
Reason 2	Recess helps improve student's performance in school.
Supporting facts	• can help student concentrate better and stay on task
	• improves memory and develops brain connections
Conclusion	Recess should be kept as part of the school day.

Conclude Your Opinion Piece

A concluding statement is often what your reader remembers best. Summarize your main points in a fresh way and use your last sentence to make a strong final impression.

Reread and Proofread

Reread your writing to check that your opinion piece is clear and your reasons are logically organized. Also proofread for errors. Make any changes that are needed.

Use the following questions to guide your revision.

- ☐ Does my response answer all parts of the prompt?
- ☐ Is my point of view clearly stated?
- ☐ Do I use enough reasons, facts, and details to support my point of view?
- ☐ Is my writing well organized and focused?
- ☐ Is my writing free of grammar and spelling errors?

Language Spotlight • Perfect Tense

The **tense** of a verb shows when an action happens. The **perfect tense** shows action already completed or to be completed. The chart below explains when and how to use perfect tense. On a separate sheet of paper, write additional examples for each.

Tense	Example
Present Perfect • tells about an action that happened at an unspecified time in the past and may still be happening now • formed by using the helping verb *has* or *have* and the past participle of the main verb	He has walked there before. You have walked there before. They have walked there before.
Past Perfect • tells about an action that was completed before some other action in the past • formed by using the helping verb *had* and the past participle of the main verb	He had walked a mile before Dad picked him up.
Future Perfect • tells about an action that will be completed at a specific time in the future • formed by using the helping verb *will have* and the past participle of the main verb	By the end of the hike, he will have walked 20 miles.

Read the passage.

Curfews for Children

Children often think that evening is the time when fun things happen. Many older children enjoy spending time with friends and attending events in the evening. On the other hand, parents usually want their children in at a "reasonable" hour. Clearly there are two sides to the issue of curfews.

A curfew is something parents use to try to keep their children safe by limiting their exposure to nighttime dangers. Parents reason that the later a child is out, the more chance that child has of getting into trouble. Parents may worry about car accidents and drivers who may be tired and careless at the end of a long day.

In addition, a curfew helps parents ensure that their children get enough sleep. This is important because children need to stay alert the next day while at school and during other activities, such as homework and afterschool sports. According to the National Sleep Foundation, children ages five to twelve need ten to eleven hours of sleep each night.

On the other hand, children may argue that their parents haven't considered their needs when making decisions about curfews. They may feel their parents do not respect their ability to make good decisions on their own. Curfews that are made without the input of the children affected may even cause children to act out in response.

What is the solution? A compromise between parents and children may be the best way to solve the curfew problem. Parents may insist that their children have a curfew. But if those children are able to be a part of the decision, there may be less conflict and more acceptance of the curfew.

Parents simply want their children safe and well rested. Children may have good suggestions about how to achieve these goals. A decision that is made by both parents and children can teach children how to problem-solve and be considerate of others' views and can give parents the control they need.

Answer the questions.

1 Which sentence gives the author's point of view on the topic of curfews?

A. Parents usually want their children in at a "reasonable" hour.

B. According to the National Sleep Foundation, children ages five to twelve need ten to eleven hours of sleep each night.

C. Children may argue that their parents haven't considered their needs when making decisions about curfews.

D. A compromise between parents and children may be the best way to solve the curfew problem.

> **Hint** Remember that an author's point of view is his or her personal belief about a topic.

2 The following question has two parts. First, answer Part A. Then, answer Part B.

Part A

Read the following excerpt from the passage. Circle the transition word or phrase.

> **In addition, a curfew helps parents ensure that their children get enough sleep. This is important since children need to stay alert the next day while at school and during other activities, such as homework and afterschool sports. According to the National Sleep Foundation, children ages five to twelve need ten to eleven hours of sleep each night.**

Part B

Explain how the author uses the transition you circled in Part A to connect his or her ideas.

_____

_____

_____

_____

> **Hint** Remember that writers use transition words or phrases to connect ideas.

3 Which of the following is a reason the author gives for why parents want curfews for their children? Circle **all** that apply.

A. They want their children in at a "reasonable" hour.

B. They do not respect their children's ability to make good decisions.

C. They want to limit children's exposure to nighttime dangers.

D. They want to keep their children from acting out.

E. They want to make sure their children get enough sleep.

F. They want to restrict their children's evening fun.

> **Hint** A reason answers the question "Why?" Think about the reasons stated in the passage that are from the parents' point of view.

4 Read the following fact.

> **According to the National Highway Traffic Safety Administration, 49 percent of fatal crashes happen at night, which is about three times as high as during daytime hours.**

The writer wants to add that fact to the passage. Where in the passage is the **best** place to add this information?

A. In paragraph 1 after the sentence, "On the other hand, parents usually want their children in at a 'reasonable' hour."

B. In paragraph 2 after the sentence, "Parents reason that the later a child is out, the more chance that child has of getting into trouble."

C. In paragraph 2 after the sentence, "Parents may worry about car accidents and drivers who may be tired and careless at the end of a long day."

D. In paragraph 3 after the sentence, "In addition, a curfew helps parents ensure that their children get enough sleep."

> **Hint** Writers use facts and details to support their reasons. Which reason does this fact support?

Use the Reading Guide to help you understand the passage.

Children Don't Need Curfews

Reading Guide

How can you tell what the writer's opinion is?

How does the writer structure the reasons? Is the structure logical? How can you tell?

Which details back up each reason?

Many children today have evening curfews. They have to be at home each evening by a certain time no matter what they are doing. But I believe evening curfews are unfair, unnecessary, and disrespectful to children.

Most children in grade five and up need to be out at least a few evenings a week. They often have extracurricular activities that both children and their parents feel are important. Maybe they have basketball practice that ends at 7:30 or a dance class that is dismissed at 8:00. These children have made commitments. Keeping these commitments may require them to be away from home in the evening. They cannot keep their commitments if they have a curfew.

Other children may have reasons to be out in the evening that are just as compelling. They may go to the library to do research for a school project. Some children may spend time studying at a friend's house. If these children had curfews, they couldn't do these activities that benefit their performance in school.

Another reason for not having a curfew is that relaxed rules help children develop good judgment on their own. They learn good judgment when they are allowed to make their own decisions and their own mistakes. Children also develop good judgment when parents help them learn how to handle different situations. A discussion about what children should do in an emergency or when approached by a stranger can prepare children and help them make good choices. Imposing a curfew will not.

Reading Guide

How do transitions link the different viewpoints?

What point of view opposes the author's position? How does the author respond?

How does the last paragraph pull together the ideas in the passage?

When children do not have a curfew, they need to develop responsibility. If they are allowed to stay out in the evening, they should also take responsibility for themselves. They should make sure they get enough sleep, get themselves up in the morning, get to school on time, and do their homework. If children are responsible, as I am, and study and do their homework as they are supposed to, staying out in the evening will not cause a problem for them.

Parents worry that their children will be unsafe without a curfew. The earlier children are in for the evening, they think, the less chance they have of getting into a dangerous situation. Parents worry about their children having accidents in the evening. Many car accidents occur at night because drivers do not see children walking or biking in the dark.

However, parents forget that their children want to be safe, too. Children can work with their parents to avoid dangerous situations. For example, children who ride their bikes home in the evening can ride with a light so drivers will see them. Children can call their parents for a ride home if it is too dark to walk. In addition, many children have their own cell phones so they can call to check in with their parents throughout the evening. They can also use their cell phones to call a parent or the police if they need help. By taking these measures, children do not need curfews because they have planned other ways to stay safe in the evening.

Part of growing up is learning how to make decisions and become independent. This means that parents and children need to develop trust. A curfew is not the way to build trust. A better way is for parents and children to talk openly. Parents can voice their concern. Children can respond and share their point of view. Then parents and children can reach a solution that they both feel comfortable with. Open discussion between parents and children improves communication, which, in turn, leads to trust. Curfews for children should not be part of it.

Answer the following questions.

1 This question has two parts. First, answer Part A. Then, answer Part B.

Part A

Which of the following **best** describes the author's point of view?

A. Curfews for children are unnecessary.

B. Parents who want curfews don't trust their children.

C. Curfews don't keep children out of trouble.

D. Students participate in activities without curfews.

Part B

Circle **one** sentence in the passage that **best** opposes the author's point of view.

2 Write **two** supporting facts from the passage that support the reason given in the graphic organizer below.

Reason	Relaxed rules help children develop good judgment on their own.
Supporting facts	

3 Reread the concluding paragraph. Find the sentence that restates or summarizes the author's opinion.

Rewrite it on the lines.

_____

_____

_____

4 Which of the following gives a reason supporting the author's point of view about curfews? Circle **all** that apply.

A. Children can plan ways to stay safe in the evening.

B. Children lack common sense and do things that could get them into trouble.

C. Children cannot learn good judgment if they are not allowed to make their own decisions.

D. Children need to schedule school activities in the afternoon.

E. Children can be responsible and make sure their schoolwork is done.

5 The following sentence could be included in the passage. Which one shows the correct verb tense?

A. Parents will be able to trust their children if the children had demonstrated that they were responsible.

B. Parents will be able to trust their children if the children have demonstrated that they are responsible.

C. Parents are able to trust their children if the children had demonstrated that they will be responsible.

D. Parent have been able to trust their children if the children had demonstrated that they are responsible.

6 "Curfews for Children" discusses opinions and reasons both for and against curfews. "Children Don't Need Curfews" argues against curfews. Think about the opinions, reasons, facts, and details presented in both passages. Why might a child be in favor of curfews? Write an opinion piece from the point of view of a child who supports a curfew. Include information from both passages to support your opinion.

Plan your opinion piece in the space below. Write your opinion piece on the following pages.

Plan

Write your opinion piece on the lines below.

W.5.5, L.5.1.a–e, L.5.2.a–e, L.5.3.a

Revise and Edit

A writer's first draft is not the polished story or essay that people read. A **draft** is the first version of a piece of writing. To get from a draft to the final product, writers must revise and edit their work. Writers don't change and fix everything in their draft all at once. They do it step by step, beginning with the big picture and ending with the smallest details.

Revising Your Writing

Revising a draft makes it better. When you **revise**, you read your draft to see how you can improve the focus, structure, ideas, and language of your writing. Sometimes it's helpful to have someone else read your writing and offer suggestions for improvement. When you revise, consider the following aspects of your draft.

- Meaning: Is your meaning clear? Would a different approach or structure make your meaning clearer or more effective?

- Readability: Is your writing interesting enough to keep your reader reading? Does your word choice fit your audience and purpose?

- Style: Are your sentences as powerful as they can be? Is your word choice effective?

Editing for Grammar

After you revise your draft for content and organization, you should edit it for errors in grammar. One important area to review is verb tenses. The **tense** of a verb shows when an action happens. The chart on the following page shows various verb tenses and how to use them correctly.

Tense	Example
Present: • tells about an action that is happening now or happens regularly • the verb form must agree with the subject	He <u>walks</u> today. You <u>walk</u> each day. They <u>walk</u> together every day.
Past: • tells about an action that happened in the past • formed by adding –*ed* to the regular verb	He <u>walked</u> yesterday.
Future: • tells about an action that will happen • formed by using the helping verb *will* plus the main verb	He <u>will walk</u> tomorrow.
Present Perfect: • tells about an action that happened at an unspecified time in the past and may still be happening now • formed by using the helping verb *has* or *have* and the past participle of the main verb	He <u>has walked</u> there before. You <u>have walked</u> there before. They <u>have walked</u> there before.
Past Perfect: • tells about an action that was completed before some other action in the past • formed by using the helping verb *had* and the past participle of the main verb	He <u>had walked</u> a mile before Dad picked him up.
Future Perfect: • tells about an action that will be completed at a specific time in the future • formed by using the helping verb *will have* and the past participle of the main verb	By the end of the hike, he <u>will have walked</u> 20 miles.

Proofreading Your Writing

Proofread to make sure you have used standard English capitalization, punctuation, and spelling in your writing. When proofreading for punctuation, be sure to use a **comma** to:

- separate items in a series.

- separate an introductory element from the rest of the sentence.

- set off interjections, such as *yes* and *no*.

- set off a **tag question**, a statement that is turned into a question.

- indicate **direct address**, which is when the writer or a character is speaking to someone directly.

The titles of full-length works are italicized on a computer or underlined in longhand. The titles of shorter works are set off in quotation marks.

Spell all words correctly. Use references and your knowledge of spelling patterns to check your work.

Language Spotlight • Vary Sentence Style

You can make your writing more interesting and flow better by varying sentence style. For example, add details to **expand sentences**. If your writing is choppy or wordy, look for ways to **combine sentences**. **Reduce sentences** by deleting any words or sentences that are repetitive or off-topic. Read the paragraph below. How could you vary the style of the sentences to improve the paragraph?

Golden retrievers make good, wonderful pets. They are smart, gentle, and loyal. My cat is named Goldie.

This passage contains mistakes. Read the passage.

Satellites in Our Lives

(1) Turn on the television. (2) Send a text on your cell phone. (3) You take these things for granted. (4) But without satellites, you couldn't do either of them.

(5) A satellite is something that orbits, or circles, a planet or a star. (6) An artificial satellite is a machine that orbits Earth. (7) People build artificial satellites and send them into space.

(8) Artificial satellites are useful in many ways. (9) There position in space affords them a birds-eye view of large areas of Earth at one time. (10) This gives satellites the ability to gather data much more quickly than instruments on Earth. (11) They can transmit data much more quickly, too.

(12) Launched in 1957, Sputnik was the first artificial satellite. (13) In the decades since then, scientists have launched thousands of satellites. (14) The satellites orbit Earth, loaded with a variety of instruments that do different jobs. (15) Now satellites affect our lives each day.

Satellites for Communication

(16) Communication satellites send signals almost instantly between places all over the globe. (17) Television satellites send signals from central stations to your televisions. (18) Satellite phones and airplane communications use satellites to relay signals from one device to another. (19) Banks use satellites in processing credit cards and running automated teller machines.

Satellites for Observation

(20) Scientists use observation satellites to monitor and collect information about Earth. (21) Satellites track the weather. (22) They look at climate changes and rising sea levels. (23) Satellites monitor forest fires and oil spills, and they help rescue teams find people in distress. (24) They had even photographed and mapped nearly every part of Earth, so you can now use the Internet to find your house.

(25) Some satellites observe space from outside Earth's atmosphere. (26) Satellite telescopes allow scientists to see black holes new planets and other space phenomena they cannot see from Earth's surface.

Satellites for Finding Our Way and Keeping Time

(27) The Global Positioning System (GPS) uses satellites to help people find their way on roads around the world. (28) But the GPS does much more than that. (29) GPS satellites are clocks in space. (30) Computer networks around the world use the GPS time clocks to coordinate their processes. (31) If the GPS failed, the timing of the processes would be off. (32) That means that the Internet would go down. (33) Around the world, electrical systems, cell phones, and many other systems would fail.

(34) When Sputnik was launched more than fifty years ago, few people could envision how satellites would change our lives. (35) Now if all the satellites went down at once, our modern life would come to an abrupt halt.

(36) What will satellites be able to do in the future? (37) No one can predict this accurately. (38) But based on the extraordinary developments of the recent past, we do know one thing: The potential for new satellite applications is vast.

Answer the following questions.

1 Read this sentence from the passage.

> **There** position in space affords them a birds-eye view of large areas of Earth at **one** time.

Which change should be made to **one** of the underlined words to correct a spelling mistake in the sentence?

A. Change "There" to "Their."

B. Change "one" to "won."

C. Change "There" to "They're."

D. Change "one" to "wun."

Hint Think about what you know about easily confused words and common spelling patterns.

---

2 Which of the following **best** combines sentences 10 and 11?

A. This gives satellites the ability to gather and transmit data much more quickly than instruments on Earth.

B. This gives satellites the ability to gather data, and they can transmit it much more quickly than instruments on Earth.

C. This gives satellites the ability to gather data and transmit it, which they can do much more quickly than instruments on Earth.

D. This gives satellites the ability to gather data much more quickly than instruments on Earth, and they can transmit it much more quickly, too.

Hint When combining sentences, look for ways to delete repeated words or information.

3 The following sentence contains errors in punctuation. Rewrite the sentence with correct punctuation.

Satellite telescopes allow scientists to see black holes new planets and other space phenomena they cannot see from Earth's surface.

_____

_____

_____

Hint Think about the rule for separating items in a series.

4 The following question has two parts. First, answer Part A. Then, answer Part B.

Part A

Read the following excerpt from the passage. Underline the sentence with an inappropriate shift in verb tense.

(20) Scientists use observation satellites to monitor and collect information about Earth. (21) Satellites track the weather. (22) They look at climate changes and rising sea levels. (23) Satellites monitor forest fires and oil spills, and they help rescue teams find people in distress. (24) They had even photographed and mapped nearly every part of Earth, so you can now use the Internet to find your house.

Part B

Rewrite the sentence you underlined in Part A, using correct verb tense.

_____

_____

Hint This question has two parts. First, decide which sentence is incorrect. Then, rewrite the sentence with any necessary corrections.

This passage contains mistakes. Use the Reading Guide to help you find the mistakes and understand the passage.

A Flight to Remember

Reading Guide

Could the author expand any sentences to add sensory details?

Would it help the flow of the writing to add transitions?

Does the author correctly indicate the title of the book?

(1) Saul's palms were sweaty as he boarded the plane. (2) He had never traveled on a plane by himself. (3) But then he thought of seeing his grandparents when he got off the plane in Newark, New Jersey, and a calming smile spread across his face. (4) Marie, the flight attendant, helped Saul stow his suitcase in the overhead compartment and get buckled in. (5) The boy settled into his seat. (6) He pulled out his tablet and headphones. (7) He planned to enjoy some movies on the five-hour flight from Phoenix. (8) If that got tiresome, he had Carl Hiaasen's book "Hoot" to read.

(9) The flight was uneventful, and Saul removed his headphones only when he felt the plane's landing gear click into place. (10) "Ladies and gentlemen," the pilot announced, "we are making our descent into Philadelphia International Airport."

(11) *What?* (12) *Did I get on the wrong plane?* Saul wondered. (13) *Why are we landing in Philadelphia?* (14) He began to panic and looked around for Marie. (15) The woman next to Saul noticed his agitation.

(16) "A thunderstorm is passing over the New York area," she explained reassuringly. (17) "We are being diverted to Philadelphia for several hours, and then they send us along to Newark."

(18) When the plane landed, Saul remained in his seat and fiddled with his tablet while Marie completed her duties on the plane.

(19) "This plane is grounded for a while," Marie informed him at last, "but they are allowing some flights into Newark, so I was able to get you on a connecting flight." (20) Marie escorted Saul off the plane and, after a long trek, they reached another airplane destined for Newark.

(21) "This is a full flight," Marie said, "but you're very fortunate because there's a seat for you in first class." (22) Marie directed Saul to his new seat and stowed his bag, but Saul couldn't move. (23) He stared at the passenger in the seat next to his. (24) Derek Jones, his favorite basketball player of all time, was stretched out in the seat next to Saul's.

(25) "Are you OK?" Marie inquired, as Saul stood transfixed in the aisle.

(26) Saul could only nod as his eyes widened and his mouth hung open. (27) His heart pounded wildly as he slid into his seat and fastened his seatbelt.

(28) "Hi, what's up?" Derek questioned. (29) "What brings you here today—business or pleasure?"

(30) Saul wasn't sure what to say. (31) "Uh, there was a storm, and, um, my plane landed. (32) But we went to the wrong airport."

(33) Saul took a calming breath, and then his enthusiasm spilled out. (34) "You're my favorite basketball star of all time. (35) You are so cool, and this is so awesome, and wait until I tell my friends who I sat next to on the plane. (36) They're never going to believe me!"

(37) "Slow down, buddy," Derek grinned. (38) "I love to meet my fans. (39) What do you think we could do so your friends will believe you?"

(40) "We could take a picture with my phone," Saul suggested. (41) "But we'll have to wait until we land."

(42) "Sounds like a plan," Derek agreed wholeheartedly.

(43) Saul cleared his throat. (44) "Mr. Jones, do you mind if I ask you about playing for the Knicks?"

(45) "Sure, ask me anything. (46) And, please, call me Derek."

Reading Guide

Are any of the sentences choppy or redundant? Could any sentences be combined?

Does the author use verb tenses correctly?

(47) The next hour in the air sped by. (48) Saul and Derek discussed and talked about basketball. (49) They talked about school. (50) They talked about college. (51) Saul's grandparents had gone to City College. (52) They shared stories about their families. (53) Too soon, the airplane landed in Newark. (54) Saul didn't want the plane ride to end.

(55) "I sure hope you can make it to a game the next time the Knicks play in Phoenix," Derek said as they gathered their belongings. (56) Saul thanked Derek as they made their way off the plane and into the terminal.

(57) "Grandma! (58) Grandpa!" Saul shouts when he saw his grandparents waiting for him. (59) "You're never going to believe who I sat next to on the plane!"

(60) "Let's see," Grandpa replied, looking over Saul's shoulder. (61) "Could it have been the one and only Derek Jones?"

(62) "How did you guess?" Saul asked, astonished. (63) Then he heard a deep voice behind him.

(64) "Saul, you almost forgot our photograph," Derek said, smiling. (65) "I think we can take that picture here."

(66) Saul beamed broadly as he and Derek posed for the picture. (67) Now he had proof that he had met Derek Jones. (68) What a story he would have to tell to his friends when he returned home!

Answer the following questions.

1 Expand sentences 5 and 6 and make them flow more smoothly by adding sensory details and transitions.

_____

_____

2 The following question has two parts. First, answer Part A. Then, answer Part B.

Part A

Which sentence has errors in punctuation?

A. He planned to enjoy some movies on the five-hour flight from Phoenix.

B. If that got tiresome, he had Carl Hiaasen's book "Hoot" to read.

C. The flight was uneventful, and Saul removed his headphones only when he felt the plane's landing gear click into place.

D. "Ladies and gentlemen," the pilot announced, "we are making our descent into Philadelphia International Airport."

Part B

Rewrite the sentence you chose in Part A, using correct punctuation.

_____

_____

3 Read the following excerpt from the passage.

> **(57) "Grandma! (58) Grandpa!" Saul shouts when he saw his grandparents waiting for him.**

Which change should be made to the underlined word to correct the verb tense?

A. will shout

B. shouted

C. had shouted

D. has shouted

4 Read the following excerpt from the passage.

> **(48) Saul and Derek discussed and talked about basketball. (49) They talked about school. (50) They talked about college. (51) Saul's grandparents had gone to City College. (52) They shared stories about their families.**

Which **best** shows how to combine the sentences?

A. Saul and Derek discussed and talked about basketball, school, and college. They shared stories about their families.

B. Saul and Derek talked about basketball, school, and college. Saul's grandparents had gone to City College. They shared stories about their families.

C. Saul and Derek discussed basketball, school, and college, and they shared stories about their families.

D. Saul and Derek discussed basketball. They talked about school and college. Then they shared stories about their families.

5 The following question has two parts. First, answer Part A. Then, answer Part B.

Part A

Read the following excerpt from the passage. Underline the sentence with an inappropriate shift in verb tense.

> **(16) "A thunderstorm is passing over the New York area," she explained reassuringly. (17) "We are being diverted to Philadelphia for several hours, and then they send us along to Newark."**
> **(18) When the plane landed, Saul remained in his seat and fiddled with his tablet while Marie completed her duties on the plane.**

Part B

Rewrite the sentence you underlined in Part A, using correct verb tense.

_____

_____

_____

6 Reread the last paragraph of "A Flight to Remember." What might Saul tell his friends about his trip and meeting Derek Jones? Write the story that Saul would tell in his voice. In your story, use details from the passage to describe what happened and what Saul thought and felt.

When you are finished, check to make sure you have followed the rules of grammar usage, punctuation, capitalization, and spelling.

Plan your story in the space below. Write your story on the following pages.

Plan

Write your story on the lines below.

Read the passage.

Women and the Revolutionary War

We tend to think only men played a role in the Revolutionary War. But women also participated in the colonies' fight for independence. During the war, women fought in battle, acted as spies, supported the troops, and ran their families' farms. They played an important role on both the American and British sides.

Only men were allowed to participate in battle. Still, some women managed to see combat. Deborah Sampson, a woman from Massachusetts, dressed as a man to fight in the war for eighteen months. To do so, she used the name Robert Shurtliff. Sampson fought in several battles in New York. She was even wounded by a saber blow to the head and a musket ball in her thigh. To keep her identity safely hidden, Sampson removed the musket ball herself and returned to the battle. After the war, she married Benjamin Gannett, a farmer, and had three children.

Women also spied for both the American and the British armies. Most men thought that women were not capable of understanding the military. As a result, it was often easier for females to gain access to opposing camps. "Miss Jenny," whose real name was never uncovered, spied on French troops for the British. At one point, she was captured by the Americans and questioned by General George Washington, who later returned her to the French. Another woman, Ann Bates, spied for the British by posing as a peddler selling items to American troops.

Large numbers of women and their children lived as camp followers behind the lines of the battles. These women followed their husbands during the war and performed jobs to help the troops. In exchange for food rations, camp followers often washed the troops' laundry, mended their clothes, and cooked meals for them. Even though these women earned food rations, they often charged soldiers money for doing these jobs. One well-known camp follower was Mary Ludwig Hayes. Her husband, John, was a soldier in Pennsylvania. During at least one battle, Hayes helped her husband and other soldiers by bringing drinking water to the battlefield. She even took over firing a cannon when her husband was too ill to do so. According to some historians, she may be the real-life woman on whom the legend of Molly Pitcher is based.

Women also worked as nurses tending to sick and injured soldiers. During the Revolutionary War, Congress allowed one male or female nurse for every ten soldiers. Hiring women as nurses freed men to fight on the front lines. In exchange for their service, nurses were paid between four and eight dollars a month. Nursing brought its share of risks, however. Nurses were constantly exposed to viruses, infections, and diseases. They faced other dangers, too. Hannah Blair, a woman from North Carolina, nursed wounded soldiers. A patriot sympathizer, she brought medicine, food, and water to American soldiers and even hid a few in her home. Eventually, the British discovered what she was doing and burned her farm to the ground.

While some women stayed close to the battles, others chose to remain at home on the family farm. With their husbands away, these women raised their children, planted and harvested crops, and even ran their husbands' businesses. Throughout the war, women dealt with shortages of goods and a lack of money. In response, they often improvised by using thorns instead of pins and making tea from local plants. They also had to be on alert constantly for troops and battles nearby. Looters or thieves sometimes tried to take advantage of a woman living alone with her children.

While the contributions of numerous women have been lost to history, we still know a great deal about how some women contributed to the war effort. Whether they fought in battle, worked as spies, followed their husbands during the war, or tended the home front, colonial women played an integral role in America's victory in the Revolutionary War.

Answer the following questions.

1 This question has two parts. First, answer part A. Then, answer part B.

Part A

Which of the following would make the **best** topic sentence for a summary of the passage?

- **A.** Some women did dangerous jobs during the Revolutionary War.
- **B.** Many women stayed home so their husbands could fight in the Revolutionary War.
- **C.** Women played many different roles during the Revolutionary War.
- **D.** Some women were camp followers during the Revolutionary War.

Part B

Underline the sentence from the passage that **best** supports your answer to Part A.

2 This question has two parts. First, answer Part A. Then, answer Part B.

Part A

Read the excerpt from the passage. Circle the transition.

> **In exchange for food rations, camp followers often washed the troops' laundry, mended their clothes, and cooked meals for them. Even though these women earned food rations, they often charged soldiers money for doing these jobs.**

Part B

How does the transition you circled connect ideas?

- **A.** It indicates that women earned food rations before they charged soldiers money to do jobs like laundry, mending, and cooking.
- **B.** It indicates that women who earned food rations would not have been expected to charge money to do certain jobs.
- **C.** It indicates a similarity between earning food rations and charging money to do certain jobs.
- **D.** It indicates that earning food rations caused women to charge money to do certain jobs.

3 This question has two parts. First, answer Part A. Then, answer Part B.

Part A

Which of the following opinions could **best** be supported with at least one detail from "Women and the Revolutionary War"? Choose **all** that apply.

A. The U.S. government should issue a stamp to honor the contributions of women in wartime.

B. Camp followers did not deserve to receive rations.

C. Overall, women were more successful at nursing than men during the war.

D. Soldiers who fought in the Revolution were not paid enough.

E. During the Revolution, women should have been permitted to fight in combat.

F. Without the help of women, the American side would likely still have won the war.

Part B

Write **one** reason to support each opinion you chose in Part A. Then cite **one** fact or detail from the passage to support each reason. Write your answer on the lines below.

_____

_____

_____

_____

_____

_____

_____

_____

Read the passage.

excerpted from

Familiar Letters of John Adams and His Wife Abigail Adams, During the Revolution

During the Revolutionary War, many women struggled to manage both family and farm during their husbands' absences. Letters between Abigail Adams and her husband, John, shine a light on the struggles that women endured. In 1774, John Adams left his family's farm in Braintree, Massachusetts, to serve as a delegate to the First Continental Congress in Philadelphia. Later, he spent time in the Second Continental Congress and worked as a diplomat to England and France. This absence resulted in a wealth of letters between husband and wife. The letters of Abigail Adams provide a glimpse into the lives of everyday women during the Revolutionary War.

In this letter, Abigail Adams provides her husband with updates regarding the Revolutionary War as it approaches their home near Boston, Massachusetts.

Braintree, 24 May, 1775.

I suppose you have had a formidable account of the alarm we had last Sunday morning. When I rose, about six o'clock, I was told that the drums had been some time beating, and that three alarm guns were fired. . . . I immediately sent off an express to know the occasion, and found the whole town in confusion. Three sloops and one cutter had come out and dropped anchor just below Great Hill. It was difficult to tell their designs; some supposed they were coming to Germantown, others to Weymouth; people, women, children, from the iron-works, came flocking down this way; every woman and child driven off from below my father's; my father's family flying. . . . The report was to them that three hundred had landed, and were upon their march up into town. The alarm flew like lightning, and men from all parts came flocking down, till two thousand were collected.

Yesterday we had an account of three ships coming into Boston. I believe it is true, as there was a salute from the other ships, though I have not been able to learn from whence they come.

Our house has been, upon this alarm, in the same scene of confusion that it was upon the former. Soldiers coming in for a lodging, for breakfast, for supper, for drink, etc. Sometimes refugees from Boston, tired and fatigued, seek an asylum for a day, a night, a week.

In this letter, dated two months later, Abigail Adams tells her husband about the scarcity of goods during the Revolutionary War. During that time, it was often challenging to get even the most basic goods. However, it was especially difficult to find sugar, tea, spices, and other goods normally imported into America. She also provides an update about the crops on their farm.

Braintree, 16 July, 1775.

Every article here in the West India way is very scarce and dear. In six weeks we shall not be able to purchase any article of the kind. . . . You can hardly imagine how much we want many common small articles, which are not manufactured amongst ourselves; but we will have them in time; not one pin to be purchased for love or money. I wish you could convey me a thousand by any friend travelling this way. I should have been glad to have laid in a small stock of the West India articles, but I cannot get one copper; no person thinks of paying anything, and I do not choose to run in debt. I endeavor to live in the most frugal manner possible, but I am many times distressed.

We have, since I wrote you, had many fine showers, and, although the crops of grass have been cut short, we have a fine prospect of Indian corn and English grain. We have not yet been much distressed for grain. Everything at present looks blooming. Oh that peace would once more extend her olive branch!

I hope to hear from you soon. Do let me know if there is any prospect of seeing you. Next Wednesday is thirteen weeks since you went away. I must bid you adieu.

Answer the following questions.

4 This question has two parts. First, answer Part A. Then, answer Part B.

Part A

Jordan would like to use evidence from Abigail Adams's letters in a report on how military blockades reduced the availability of imported goods during the American Revolution. Underline details from "Familiar Letters of John Adams and His Wife Abigail Adams, During the Revolution" that Jordan might use.

Part B

In a few sentences, paraphrase the information you underlined. Write your answer on the lines below.

_____

_____

_____

5 This question has two parts. First, answer Part A. Then, answer Part B.

Part A

Read the facts about Abigail Adams. Circle the fact that **best** explains why the author of "Women and the Revolutionary War" might include Adams's letters in the passage.

Abigail Adams was married to a well-known patriot.
Abigail Adams ran her family's farm during the war.
Abigail Adams updated her husband about how the war affected their home.

Part B

Circle the paragraph in "Women and the Revolutionary War" in which the author would **most** likely use the fact you circled to develop the topic. Then write a sentence showing how you would include the information in that paragraph.

_____

_____

_____

6 This question has two parts. First, answer Part A. Then, answer Part B.

Part A

The sentences below are from a student's research paper on the life of Abigail Adams. If a sentence contains mistakes, rewrite it correctly on the line. If a sentence is written correctly, write "correct" on the line.

A. The couple was married in 1764 and moved to Braintree, MA.

_____

B. After they are married John will work towards a career in law while Abigail ran they're household.

_____

C. Even though Adams has not received a formal education she still enjoyed reading.

_____

D. Reading created a bond between her and John Adams, a Harvard iaw graduate.

_____

E. She spent hours in her father's library and she read Shakespeare plays like Romeo and Juliet.

_____

Part B

Reorder the sentences so that they form a clear and logical paragraph. Write the letters of the sentences ordered correctly in the boxes below.

☐ ☐ ☐ ☐ ☐

PERFORMANCE TASK

As you've learned, women played a number of roles during the Revolutionary War. Decide which role you think most impacted the outcome of the war, and write an essay that explains your reasoning. Use evidence from "Women and the Revolutionary War" and "Familiar Letters of John Adams and His Wife Abigail Adams, During the Revolution" to support your point of view.

Use the space below to plan your writing.

Plan

Write your response on the lines below.

Listening

SL.5.2, L.5.4.c

Listen to Literature

1 GETTING THE IDEA

Literature is a written work, such as a novel, short story, play, or poem. People read aloud works of literature to entertain their audiences. As a student, you probably often listen to a classmate, teacher, or librarian read aloud a piece of literature. You might also listen to literature through an audio or video recording.

Listening to Literature
Regardless of how the literature is presented, listen carefully in order to:

- identify the main story elements, including characters, setting, point of view, theme, and plot.

- identify details about the story elements.

- summarize the piece of literature.

Notes As you listen, take notes to help you remember what you hear. Taking notes doesn't mean writing down every word you hear or writing in complete sentences. Instead, jot down names, places, key words, and ideas. Use abbreviations or draw sketches and arrows to help you remember connections between characters and plot events. Remember that your notes are just for you. They don't have to be neat, but you do need to be able to read your writing. Your notes should help you get the most from a story.

Graphics Graphics, or visuals, are an important part of many presentations. Pay attention to any graphics, such as illustrations, that are included. They might explain parts of the story or provide additional information for you to consider.

First Listen

Your teacher may read aloud a piece of literature more than once. You can understand the story better if you listen for different things during each reading. During the first listen, take notes only on the most important elements of the story: the characters, setting, point of view, plot events, and theme. You could make a story map before listening and use it to take notes. Don't try to write down all the details at once. But do jot down questions you have about what you hear. During the second reading, listen for the answers to those questions. The chart below lists elements to listen for during the first listen.

First Listen		
Element	**Ask Yourself**	**Listen For**
characters	Who are the characters? Who is the focus of story?	• the characters' names • clues about the characters through dialogue or description
setting	When and where does the story take place?	• place names • dates • clues that show a change in time • clues that suggest a different time period
point of view	Who is telling the story?	• first-person or third-person pronouns
plot events	What happens in the story? What is the main character's problem?	• clues about the character's conflict • how the conflict is resolved
theme	How do the characters respond to challenges?	• details about what the characters say and do

Second Listen

Review your notes before the second listen. Then during the second listen, pay attention to the details that support what you already learned about the story elements.

Second Listen		
Element	**Ask Yourself**	**Listen For**
characters	What is each character like? What does each character want?	• details about characters' thoughts and actions • details about characters' reactions to other characters and events
setting	Is the setting important to how the plot unfolds?	• clues in the words that characters use
point of view	How does the point of view affect how the story is told?	• whether the story tells the thoughts and feelings of one or more characters
theme	What message does the author want me to understand?	• what the characters learn by the end of the story
plot	How do the characters try to solve the problem?	• details about how characters' actions lead to the resolution

After Listening

After the second listen, write a summary of the story in your notes. That will help you keep the most important parts of the story in mind.

Language Spotlight • Consult References

Reference sources include print and digital dictionaries, thesauruses, and glossaries that can help you find or clarify the exact meanings of words and phrases. Read the following sentence.

The army <u>stormed</u> the fort.

Look up *storm* in a reference source. Which meaning makes sense in the sentence above?

Listen to the passage your teacher reads aloud and study the picture. Take notes in the space below. Then answer the questions.

A Field Trip to Atlantis

Notes

1 Which detail shows that the passage is science fiction? Choose **all** that apply.

A. Usually field trips were boring visits to museums or time traveling back to the dullest eras in history.

B. Caitlyn's class had spent the week before their trip studying Atlantis.

C. "Please stay together, class," said their teacher, Mrs. Rowe, as they began their tour.

D. Although Atlantis was underwater, the city was encased in a bubble filled with air.

E. Her teacher saw Caitlyn's thoughts on her mind-screen and said, "Yes, although the air is recycled, the gases are perfectly balanced for us."

> **Hint** Think about what you know about science fiction. What clues tell you when and where the story takes place? How can these clues help you answer this question?

2 The following question has two parts. First, answer Part A. Then, answer Part B.

Part A

Which word describes Caitlyn? Choose **all** that apply.

A. curious   **D.** bored

B. enthusiastic   **E.** unrealistic

C. shy   **F.** clever

Part B

Choose **one** word from the answer to Part A. Explain why this word describes Caitlyn. Use details from the passage to support your answer.

_____

_____

_____

_____

> **Hint** How are Caitlyn's thoughts and actions described? What do these details tell you about Caitlyn?

3 What would the passage be about if it were told from Layla's point of view?

A. a visit by a class from above the sea

B. what sunlight is like

C. the tour of Atlantis's main power plant

D. a trip to stay with a family above the sea

Hint Think about how Layla's life is different from Caitlyn's life. How would this affect Layla's point of view?

4 In three sentences, write a summary of the passage.

_____

_____

_____

_____

_____

Hint A summary includes only the most important details. Think about what happens in the beginning, middle, and end of the story.

Use the Listening Guide to help you understand the passage your teacher reads aloud and study the drawing. Take notes in the space below.

Listening Guide

What is the point of view of the passage? How do you know? How does this point of view help you understand the characters?

Which plot events could happen in real life? Which could not?

How can you clarify the meaning of an unknown word?

What is the message the author wants listeners to understand?

The Luck of the Irish

Notes

Answer the following questions.

1 This question has two parts. First, answer Part A. Then, answer Part B.

Part A

Who is the main character?

A. Byrne

B. Cullen

C. Ryan

D. Grandpa Colm

Part B

Explain how you determined the answer to Part A. Use details from the passage to support your answer.

_____

_____

_____

2 Write a summary of "The Luck of the Irish."

_____

_____

_____

_____

3 The following question has two parts. First, answer Part A. Then, answer Part B.

Part A

Read the following excerpt from the passage.

> **The mayor was finishing his speech, thanking the <u>anonymous</u> donors who had funded the community project. "Although we may never know their names, this soccer field is a tribute to their generosity."**

Which word **best** defines <u>anonymous</u>?

A. unknown   **C.** similar

B. opposite   **D.** mysterious

Part B

Which is the **best** resource you could use to clarify the meaning of <u>anonymous</u>?

A. encyclopedia   **C.** dictionary

B. Web site   **D.** thesaurus

4 The following question has two parts. First, answer Part A. Then, answer Part B.

Part A

Which of the following **best** states the theme of the passage?

A. Finding money will help you get what you want.

B. Your friends are there to help you get what you want.

C. There is always some truth in old stories.

D. If you have more than you need, you should share with others.

Part B

Explain how you determined the answer to Part A. Use details from the passage to support your answer.

_____

_____

_____

_____

5 Write at least **one** paragraph that explains how the setting of "The Luck of the Irish" affects the plot of the story and what the characters do. Use details from the passage to support your response.

Write your answer on the lines below.

_____

_____

_____

_____

_____

_____

_____

_____

_____

_____

_____

_____

_____

_____

_____

SL.5.2, SL.5.3, L.5.5.c

Listen to Presentations

Whenever you listen to a classmate's report, a speaker at a school assembly, or your teacher presenting a lesson, you are listening to a presentation. A **presentation** is a talk, speech, or media display meant to entertain, give information, or offer a position on a topic.

Listening to a Presentation
The speaker in a presentation may be directly in front of you. For example, you may be asked to listen as your teacher reads a passage aloud. At other times, you might use a computer to play an audio recording or a video presentation.

Notes As you listen to a presentation, take notes to help you remember what you hear. You don't need to write every word you hear or write in complete sentences. Instead, jot down key words and ideas. Use abbreviations or draw sketches and arrows to help you remember connections between ideas.

Graphics Pay attention to any graphics, such as photographs, maps, charts, or graphs, that are included in a presentation. They might help explain the topic or provide additional information for you to consider.

First Listen
You may have the opportunity to listen to a presentation more than once. During the first listen, take notes on the presentation's main idea and structure. Don't try to write down all the details during this listen. Jot down questions you have about what you hear.

Listen for Main Idea and Details Identify the speaker's topic, the main points he or she makes about the topic, and how those main points are supported. Ask yourself:

- What is this presentation mostly about?

- What details, reasons, and evidence support the main points?

- Often, the main idea is reflected in the title of the presentation and discussed in the introduction. The speaker will likely restate the main idea in the conclusion.

Listen for Structure Like informative texts, an oral presentation is organized with a certain structure. The structure helps the listener connect ideas and better understand how parts of the presentation relate to the whole.

Structure	Ask Yourself	Listen For
chronological or sequential	Does the presentation tell about events in the order they happened or explain a series of steps?	dates and time-order words such as *first, next, last*
cause and effect	Does the presentation explain why something happened or describe the results of an event?	signal words such as *because, since, therefore*
problem and solution	Does the presentation describe a difficult situation and offer ways to handle it?	clue words such as *problem, challenge, obstacle, solution, resolution*
compare and contrast	Does it describe two or more ideas and point out similarities and differences between them?	signal words such as *alike, same, both, different, however*

Second Listen

Before you listen to the presentation a second time, review your notes. Then, during the second listen, pay attention to the speaker's key points, the details, examples, and reasons and evidence he or she uses to support the main idea.

Second Listen		
Elements	**Ask Yourself**	**Listen For**
key points	Does the speaker identify points directly?	phrases such as *My first point is*, *It's important to remember that*
details	Which idea does this detail support?	phrases such as *in addition*, *besides*, *as well*
examples	How does this example help me better understand a key point?	phrases such as *for example*, *is a kind of*
reasons and evidence	Does this detail tell me why? Does it show proof by giving facts?	phrases such as *one reason is*, *because*, *this shows that*, *therefore*

After the Presentation

Once you have listened to the presentation a second time, summarize it in your own words. Write the summary in your notes. That will help you remember the most important parts of the presentation.

Language Spotlight • Homographs

Homographs are words that are spelled alike but have different meanings. Some homographs have different pronunciations. Read the following sentences aloud. The underlined words are homographs. How are their meanings different? Which homographs have different pronunciations?

I <u>can</u> open a <u>can</u> of juice.

We <u>record</u> our observations so we have a <u>record</u> of what happened.

Duplication any part of this book is prohibited by law. © 2015 Triumph Learning, LLC

Listen to the passage your teacher reads aloud and study the map. Take notes in the space below. Then answer the questions.

A Lost Ancient City Is Found

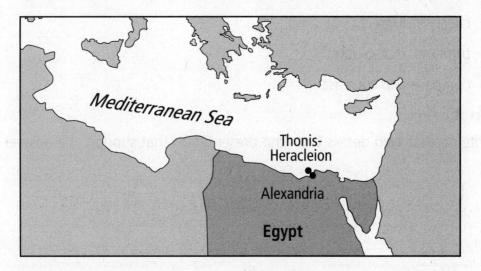

Notes

Answer the following questions.

1 This question has two parts. First, answer Part A. Then, answer Part B.

Part A

How is the presentation structured?

A. chronological order

B. cause and effect

C. problem and solution

D. compare and contrast

Part B

Write at least **two** details from the presentation that support the answer to Part A.

_____

_____

_____

> **Hint** Think about the clue words or signal words for each type of structure. Which ones did you hear most often in the presentation?

2 Before the year 2000, people thought that a port city at the mouth of the Nile River was just a legend. Write **two** reasons from the presentation that explain why people thought this way.

_____

_____

_____

> **Hint** What was the source of the account of the port city by the Nile River? Why was this source unreliable?

3 Describe **two** facts scientists have learned about Thonis-Heracleion.

_____

_____

_____

> **Hint** Think about the artifacts Goddio and his team found. What do these artifacts suggest about Thonis-Heracleion?

4 Which sentence **best** summarizes the presentation?

A. The discovery of Thonis-Heracleion proved that Herodotus's accounts were accurate.

B. Franck Goddio accidentally discovered Thonis-Heracleion, and now he wants to find out why it sank.

C. The artifacts from Thonis-Heracleion are helping scientists figure out what life there was like more than 2,300 years ago.

D. The discovery of artifacts proves that the ancient city of Thonis-Heracleion did exist, and research continues to find out more about the city and why it sank.

> **Hint** While all the answer choices may be true statements about the presentation, which one gives the most complete summary of what you heard?

Use the Listening Guide to help you understand the passage your teacher reads aloud and study the picture. Take notes in the space below.

Listening Guide

What purpose does the speaker have for giving the presentation? How do you know?

What is bioluminescence? How does knowing the meaning of this word help you understand important facts about fireflies?

Why do fireflies flash? How does it help them survive?

What is this presentation mostly about?

Flashing Fireflies: The Science Behind the Magic

Notes

Answer the following questions.

1 This question has two parts. First, answer Part A. Then, answer Part B.

Part A

What is the main purpose of the presentation?

A. to explain bioluminescence

B. to describe how fireflies produce their own light

C. to give information about fireflies

D. to persuade people to turn off their lights

E. to describe the colors and patterns of fireflies' flashing

Part B

Write at least **two** details from the presentation that support the answer to Part A.

_____

_____

2 What does the speaker mean by saying that it's almost magical to watch fireflies?

A. Fireflies use magic to produce light.

B. The way that fireflies light up a yard at night is unusually beautiful.

C. Scientists are researching whether fireflies are magic.

D. People don't know much about fireflies, so they assume that their flashing lights are magic.

3 Read the following sentence from the presentation.

If you were to <u>watch</u> fireflies on a warm summer evening, you might find it magical.

Which definition **best** tells how <u>watch</u> is used in the presentation?

A. a timepiece worn on the wrist

B. to care for

C. to observe

D. to keep under guard

4 According to the presentation, what information can firefly flashes give?
Choose **all** that apply.

    A. where they are

    B. what kind of firefly they are

    C. that they taste bad

    D. the temperature of the air

    E. how they produce their flashes

5 In **three** sentences, write a summary of the presentation.

_____

_____

_____

_____

6 Identify **three** facts from "Flashing Fireflies: The Science Behind the Magic" that you found most interesting. Which **one** of those facts would you like to learn more about? Explain why you want to learn more about that fact and what you would do to research the topic. Cite reasons and evidence from your notes to explain your response.

Write your answer on the lines below.

_____

_____

_____

_____

_____

_____

_____

_____

_____

_____

_____

_____

_____

_____

Listen to the passage your teacher reads aloud. Think about what each character's point of view tells you about that character. Use the space below to take notes on the characters, setting, conflict, and resolution.

Notes

Answer the following questions.

1 Choose words from the box to describe Jayla at the beginning of the passage and at the end of the passage. You will not use every word.

shy	tired	surprised	bored	amazed
loud	mean	quiet	happy	interested

At the **beginning**, Jayla was	At the **end**, Jayla was

2 This question has two parts. First, answer Part A. Then, answer Part B.

Part A

Read the following sentence from the passage.

   Jayla was startled when Grandpa began to <u>row</u> back to shore for lunch.

Which definition of <u>row</u> is used in the sentence?

A. noisy argument

B. move a boat through water

C. objects in a line

D. participate in the sport of rowing

Part B

Write a sentence using the word <u>row</u> with a different definition than the one you chose in Part A.

_____

_____

3 Circle **all** the words below that describe what Jayla is referring to when she says, "There really is more going on than meets the eye."

boat	time	lake	plants
Grandma	animals	school	Grandpa

4 This question has two parts. First, answer Part A. Then, answer Part B.

Part A

Which of the following **best** states the theme of the passage?

A. The world is constantly changing.

B. Living a long time makes people wise.

C. There is often more to a situation than it appears.

D. People learn by observing others around them.

Part B

Explain how you determined the answer to Part A. Use details from the passage to support your answer.

_____

_____

_____

5 In a few sentences, write a summary of the passage.

_____

_____

_____

_____

_____

_____

_____

Listen to the passage your teacher reads aloud. Study the photograph and read the caption. Take notes in the space below.

Aurora Borealis lights up the springtime sky.

Notes

Answer the following questions.

6 This question has two parts. First, answer Part A. Then, answer Part B.

Part A

What is the main purpose of the presentation?

A. to explain what the Aurora Borealis is

B. to entertain with Aurora Borealis legends

C. to persuade people to view the Aurora Borealis

D. to describe what the Aurora Borealis looks like

Part B

Use a least **two** details from the presentation to support your answer in Part A.

_____

_____

7 This question has two parts. First, answer Part A. Then, answer Part B.

Part A

Which statement **best** summarizes the key point of the presentation?

A. People who did not understand the Aurora Borealis made up explanations for why it appeared.

B. The Aurora Borealis can keep electrical power and satellites from working properly.

C. The Aurora Borealis is a display of lights in the night sky caused by a gas cloud from the sun.

D. The Aurora Borealis appears in various shades of color that glow or appear to move.

Part B

Reread the statements you didn't choose. Circle the detail that **best** supports the key point you identified in Part A.

8 This question has two parts. First, answer Part A. Then, answer Part B.

Read the sentence from the presentation.

> **Others believed the lights were <u>an omen</u> of good or bad fortune to come.**

Part A

Which words are **best** to use in place of <u>an omen</u> without changing the meaning of the sentence?

A. a sign

B. a path

C. a door

D. a choice

Part B

Which resource is **best** to use for identifying other words to replace <u>omen</u> without changing the meaning of the sentence?

A. atlas

B. glossary

C. thesaurus

D. encyclopedia

E. almanac

9 Explain why scientists might want to study the Aurora Borealis. Use details from the presentation to support your answer.

_____

_____

_____

_____

_____

Like people living in the past, people today get to see the Aurora Borealis. Write a description of the ways in which their experiences seeing the Aurora Borealis are similar and different. Use details from the presentation to support your response.

Write your answer on the lines below.

_____

_____

_____

_____

_____

_____

_____

_____

_____

_____

_____

_____

_____

_____

_____

_____

GLOSSARY

academic vocabulary the words used across content areas, such as social studies and math, that help a reader understand the topic (Lesson 8)

act a section of a drama, sometimes made up of scenes (Lesson 3)

adage an old, familiar saying that expresses wisdom or a truth about human nature (Lesson 3)

affix a word part that is added to the beginning or end of a word, changing the meaning of the word (Lesson 5)

alliteration the repetition of consonant sounds at the beginning of words (Lesson 2)

allusion a reference to a well-known person, place, or event in history or literature (Lesson 3)

antonym a word that means the opposite of another word (Lesson 10)

article a nonfiction work based on facts, usually found online and in newspapers and magazines (Lesson 5)

audience the readers of written text, or listeners of a presentation (Lesson 11)

author's purpose the reason an author writes a text—usually to inform, entertain, or persuade the reader (Lesson 8)

bandwagon appeal a persuasive technique which implies that a point of view is correct because many people think that way (Lesson 6)

bias a belief in just one way of thinking or being (Lesson 7)

bibliography a list of the resources used for a written project (Lesson 7)

cast of characters the people in a drama (Lesson 3)

cause the reason that something happens, leading to an effect or a result (Lesson 5)

cause-and-effect structure a type of text organization that shows the relationship between causes and events (Lesson 7)

character a person, an animal, or an object that takes part in the action of a narrative (Lesson 1)

chronological order the order, or sequence, in which events happened (Lesson 5)

chronological structure a type of text organization that presents events in the order in which they happened (Lesson 7)

circle graph a circular chart divided into sections that shows the parts of a whole (Lesson 8)

claim a statement that something—such as an idea, an event, or an observation—is true (Lesson 6)

comma (,) a punctuation mark used to separate an introductory element from the rest of a sentence, to separate items in a series, to indicate direct address, and to set off a tag question or the words *yes* and *no* (Lesson 13)

compare to show the similarities between objects, ideas, people, places, events, or passages (Lesson 4)

compare-and-contrast structure a type of text organization that points out similarities and differences between two or more things or ideas (Lesson 7)

conclusion the end of a piece of writing, summing up the text's main points and often leaving the reader with something to think about (Lesson 6)

conflict a problem that the characters in a fictional narrative must solve (Lesson 1)

conjunction a word—such as *and*, *but*, or *or*— that connects two words, phrases, or clauses (Lesson 11)

context clue a word or phrase in a sentence or paragraph that helps readers determine the meaning of an unknown word (Lesson 1)

contrast to show the differences between objects, ideas, people, places, events, or passages (Lesson 4)

diagram a drawing with labels that shows the parts of an object or how something works (Lesson 8)

dialogue the words that characters speak in a text; a conversation between characters in a text (Lesson 3)

domain-specific vocabulary words used in a specific area of study, such as social studies and science (Lesson 7)

draft one of the first versions of a writer's work (Lesson 17)

drama a story that is performed on a stage by actors; a play (Lesson 3)

edit to correct mistakes in grammar, spelling, capitalization, and punctuation (Lesson 11)

effect a result of a cause (Lesson 5)

evidence information used to support a claim; proof (Lesson 5)

explanatory text see *informative text*

fact information that is true and can be proved (Lesson 6)

famous name a persuasive technique in which a celebrity's or expert's name is used to promote something (Lesson 6)

fiction a type of story about made-up people and events (Lesson 1)

figurative language a word or phrase that means something other than its dictionary definition; language that contains imagery or describes something through the use of unusual comparisons for added effect, interest, and meaning (Lesson 2)

first-person point of view the perspective of a narrator who is a character in the story and who uses the pronoun *I* (Lesson 1)

flowchart a graphic organizer that uses arrows or connecting lines to show the order of something (Lesson 7)

formal style an approach to writing that uses language common in school or business settings, in which words are used carefully and chosen for their accuracy (Lesson 15)

future tense the verb tense in which the action has not happened (Lesson 15)

generalization a broad statement that tries to sound authoritative (Lesson 6)

general-to-specific structure a type of text organization that begins with a general statement and then uses specific examples to support the statement (Lesson 8)

glossary an alphabetical list of difficult or special terms and their meanings, usually printed at the end of a book (Lesson 8)

graph a chart that shows facts or information in a visual way (Lesson 7)

graphic feature a photograph, illustration, timeline, diagram, or graph in a text (Lesson 5)

historical text nonfiction text that tells about real events or people from the past (Lesson 7)

homographs words that are spelled the same, are said differently, and have different meanings (Lesson 19)

idiom a phrase that means something different from the literal, or dictionary, meaning of the words in it (Lesson 3)

inference a conclusion that is made about a text, based on information in the text and on personal knowledge (Lesson 5)

informative text nonfiction text in which the author presents information about a specific subject (Lesson 15)

interjection a word or phrase that is used in a way that shows feeling— such as *wow* or *oh* (Lesson 11)

introduction the beginning of a piece of writing, often used to capture the reader's attention and to present the text's thesis statement, or main idea (Lesson 6)

line a row of words; the basic building block of a poem (Lesson 2)

main idea the most important idea in a piece of writing (Lesson 5)

map a visual representation of an area, showing physical features, such as cities, roads, or rivers (Lesson 7)

metaphor a type of figurative language comparing two unlike things without using the word *like* or the word *as* (Lesson 2)

model a picture or object that represents a much larger, real-life object (Lesson 8)

motivation the reason(s) that a character does something (Lesson 1)

multiple-meaning words words that are spelled the same but have more than one meaning (Lesson 4)

narrate to tell a story about a topic (Lesson 11)

narrative writing the kind of writing that tells a story (Lesson 13)

narrator the person or speaker who tells a story (Lesson 1)

nonfiction the kind of writing that describes factual information about people, places, events, and things—such as biographies, essays, speeches, and textbooks (Lesson 5)

objective point of view a perspective in which the author presents facts fairly (Lesson 7)

opinion a personal belief that cannot be proved true or false (Lesson 6)

opinion piece a type of writing in which the author states a personal belief and tries to persuade others to agree (Lesson 16)

pacing the act of controlling the pace, or rate of progress, of a fictional narrative (Lesson 13)

part-to-whole structure a text organization in which facts and details lead to one main idea or concept (Lesson 8)

past tense the verb tense in which an action has already happened (Lesson 15)

perfect tense a verb tense that shows an action that has already been completed (Lesson 16)

persuade to convince the audience to think a certain way (Lesson 11)

persuasive technique a way in which an author tries to convince readers of his or her point of view (Lesson 6)

persuasive text nonfiction text in which the author tries to get the reader to agree with his or her point of view (Lesson 6)

plagiarize to pass off someone else's work as one's own (Lesson 14)

plot the sequence of events in a story that includes the characters' actions, a conflict, and a resolution (Lesson 1)

poetry literature written in lines and stanzas, often using rhyme, rhythm, and descriptive language (Lesson 2)

point of view the perspective from which a story is told (Lesson 1); an author's attitude about what he or she is describing in nonfiction text (Lesson 6)

prefix an affix that is added to the beginning of a word, changing the word's meaning (Lesson 5)

preposition a word that links a noun or a pronoun to some other word in a sentence, often to indicate how things are related in time and space (Lesson 12)

presentation a talk or speech, in which the speaker tells a story, gives information, or talks about an experience, and which may include audiovisual support (Lesson 19)

present tense the verb tense in which the action is happening now (Lesson 15)

prewriting the first step of the writing process, in which an author decides what topic to write about and what to say (Lesson 11)

problem a difficult situation, obstacle, or challenge (Lesson 5)

problem-and-solution structure a type of text organization that states a problem and then describes its solution or possible solution (Lesson 7)

proverb an old, familiar saying that expresses wisdom or gives advice (Lesson 3)

publish to make one's work available, either in print or digitally, for others to read (Lesson 11)

purpose see *author's purpose*

reason a supporting idea that explains why readers should believe an author's point of view (Lesson 6)

relevant evidence information that is directly related to a topic and supports a statement or position (Lesson 6)

repetition the repeating of a word, phrase, or line in a poem (Lesson 2)

research to gather information from sources such as books, Web sites, and newspapers; also, the process of finding facts and information in various sources (Lesson 14)

response to literature a type of writing in which a writer describes and analyzes some aspect of a literary work (Lesson 12)

revise to make corrections and changes to a draft or other piece of writing (Lesson 17)

rhyme a device in which words end with the same sound (Lesson 2)

rhyme scheme the pattern of rhyme in a poem (Lesson 2)

rhythm the beat, or pattern of stressed and unstressed syllables, in a line of poetry (Lesson 2)

scene a section of a drama, usually a smaller section within an act (Lesson 3)

sensory detail the use of words to tell how things look, feel, taste, smell, and sound (Lesson 13)

sequence the order in which events happen; also called chronological order (Lesson 5)

sequential structure text organization in which ideas and concepts are presented in the order in which they happen (Lesson 8)

setting the location and time in which a story takes place (Lesson 1)

simile a type of figurative language in which two unlike things are compared by using the word *like* or the word *as* (Lesson 2)

solution the way in which a problem is resolved (Lesson 5)

source an accurate, relevant, and credible book, Web site, or other reference material that a writer consults while doing research (Lesson 14)

spatial structure text organization in which things are described according to their location—such as a description (Lesson 8)

speaker the narrator in a poem (Lesson 2)

stage directions actions performed by characters, often written in italics (Lesson 3)

stanza a series of lines that makes up a section of a poem (Lesson 2)

structure the pattern or organization of a text (Lesson 5)

style an author's word choice, language, and sentence construction (Lesson 4)

subjective point of view a perspective in which the author uses facts based on his or her personal opinions in order to influence the reader (Lesson 7)

suffix an affix that is added to the end of a word, changing the word's meaning (Lesson 5)

summarize to retell the main points or plot of a text in one's own words (Lesson 5)

synonym a word that has the same or a similar meaning as another word (Lesson 10)

table a graphic representation that uses columns and rows to organize information (Lesson 8)

tag question a statement that is turned into a question—such as *You're going to the party, aren't you?* (Lesson 17)

text feature a format, such as bold print and a heading, used to present information in an organized way (Lesson 5)

text structure the way in which a text is organized, such as by sequence, cause and effect, or comparing and contrasting (Lesson 7)

theme the message or truth about life that a story or poem suggests (Lesson 1)

third-person point of view the perspective of a narrator who is not a character in the story and who uses the pronouns *he*, *she*, and *they* (Lesson 1)

timeline a graphic that shows the dates when important things happened in a certain time period (Lesson 7)

topic sentence a sentence that states the central idea of a text (Lesson 15)

trait a detail about a character's physical appearance or personality (Lesson 1)

transition a connecting word or phrase that enables writing to flow smoothly from one idea to the next (Lesson 9)

verb a word or words that show action or state of being (Lesson 15)

verb tense the time—past, present, or future—depicted by a verb's form (Lesson 15)